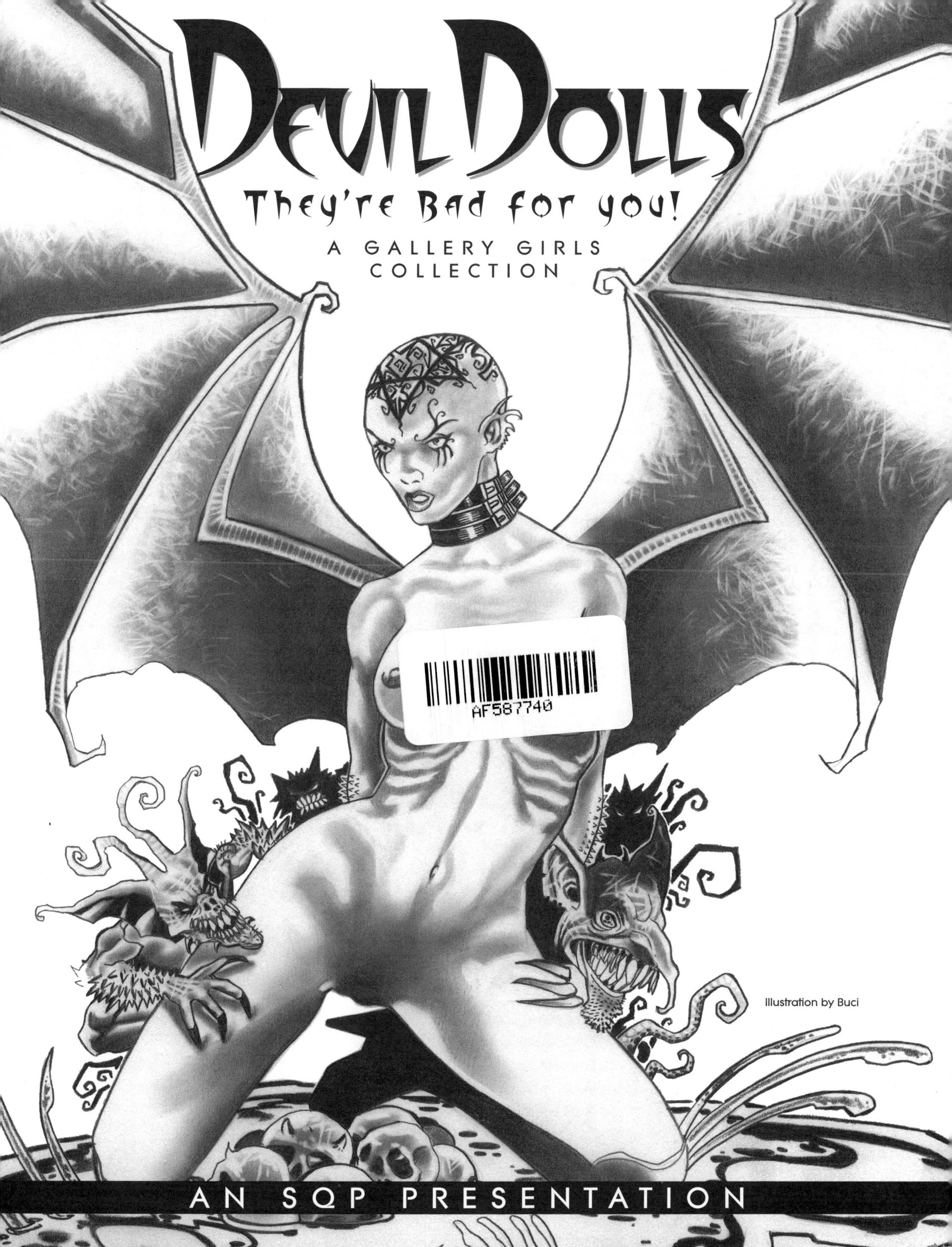

Illustration by Buci

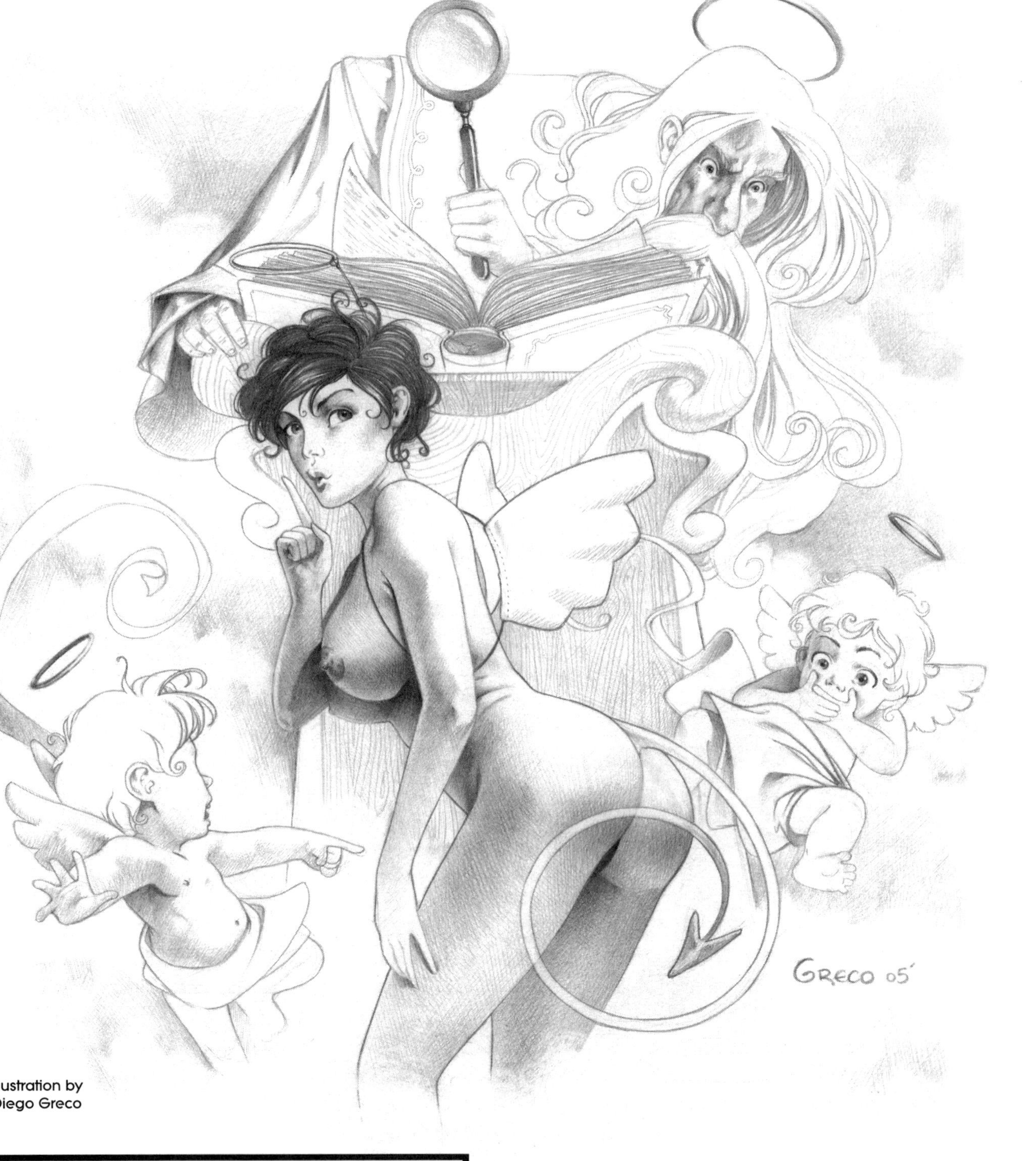

Illustration by
Diego Greco

DEVIL DOLLS

Volume One

 Printed in the United States.
Book design by Grassy Knoll Studios.

Published by
SQP Inc.
PO Box 248 - Columbus, NJ 08022

Sal Quartuccio & Bob Keenan - Publishers

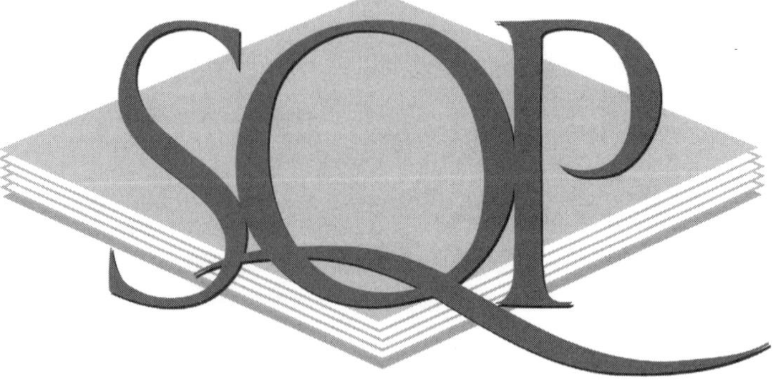

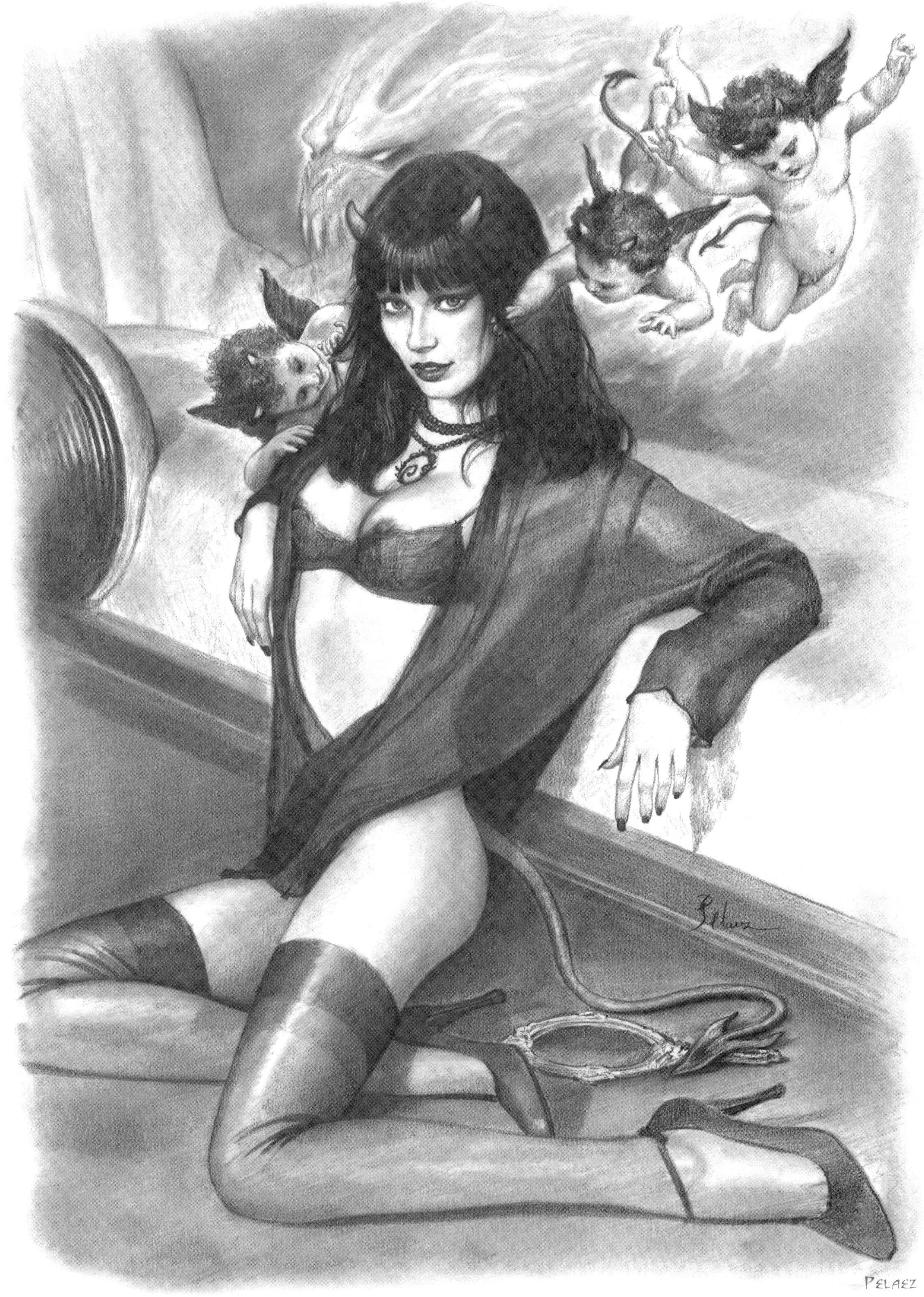

PELAEZ

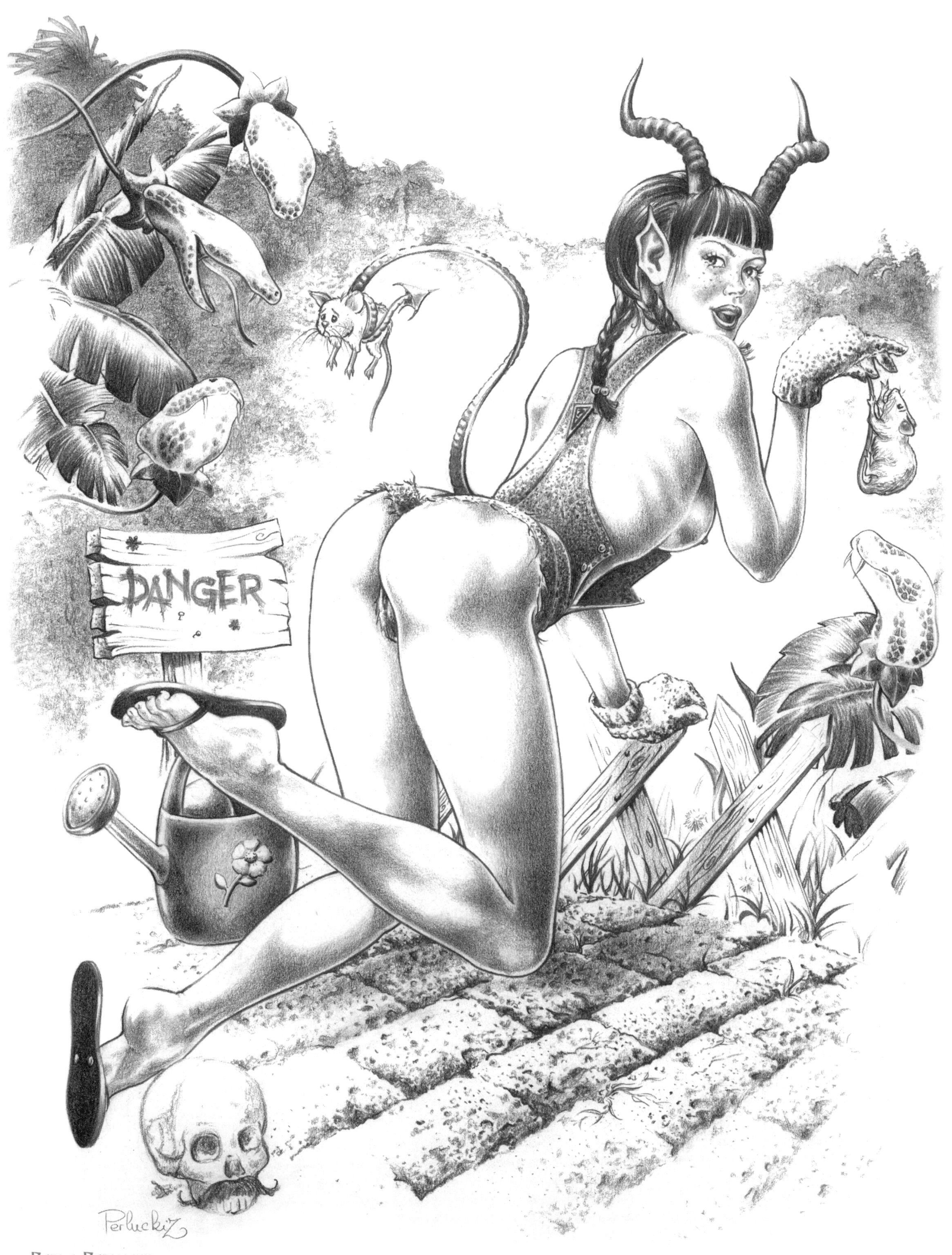

Perla Perlucky

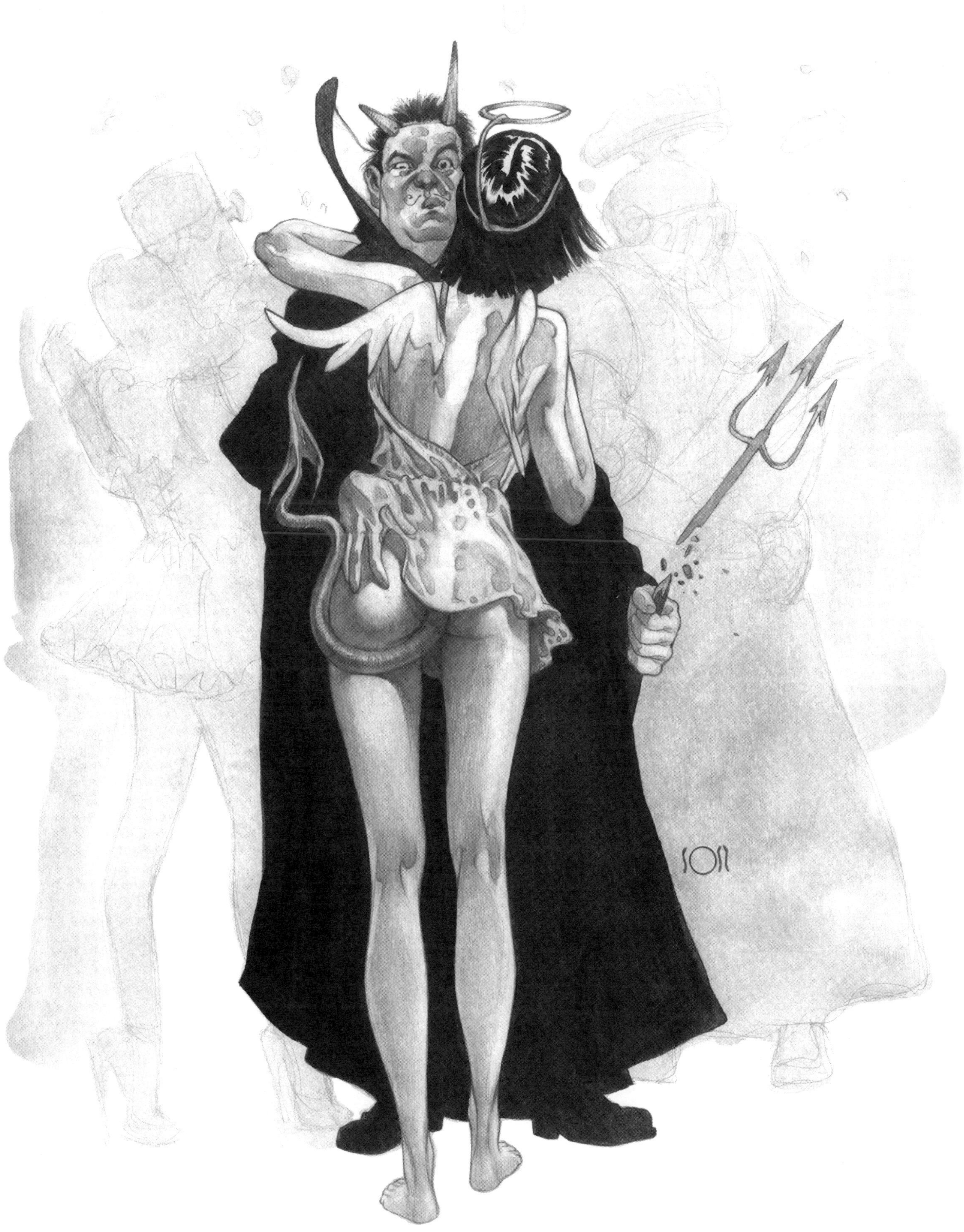

Marcelo Sosa

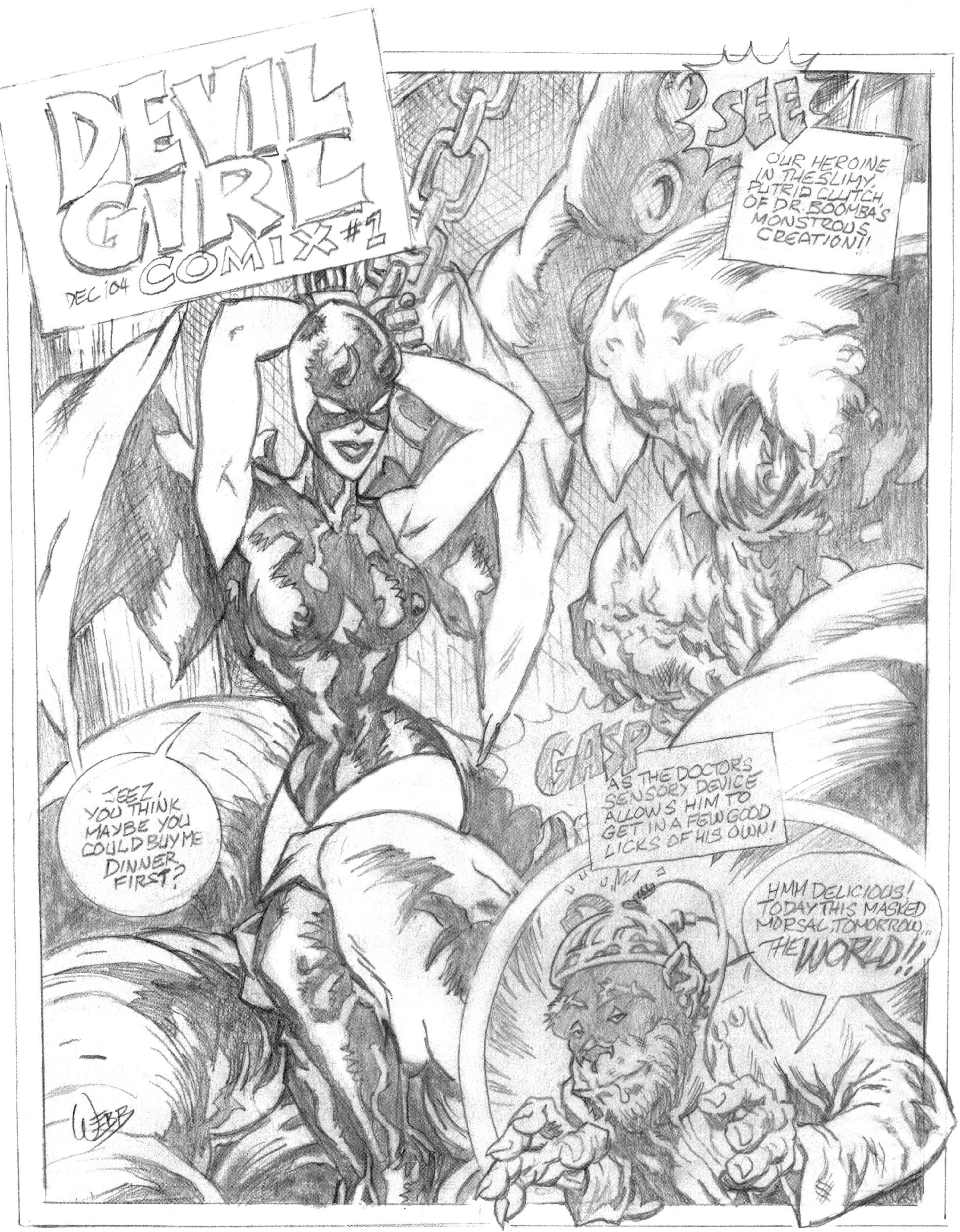
DEVIL GIRL COMIX #1
DEC '04
SEEZ
OUR HEROINE IN THE SLIMY, PUTRID CLUTCH OF DR. BOOMBA'S MONSTROUS CREATION!!
GASP
AS THE DOCTORS SENSORY DEVICE ALLOWS HIM TO GET IN A FEW GOOD LICKS OF HIS OWN!
JEEZ, YOU THINK MAYBE YOU COULD BUY ME DINNER FIRST?
HMM DELICIOUS! TODAY THIS MASKED MORSAL, TOMORROW... THE WORLD!!
WEBB

Jim Webb

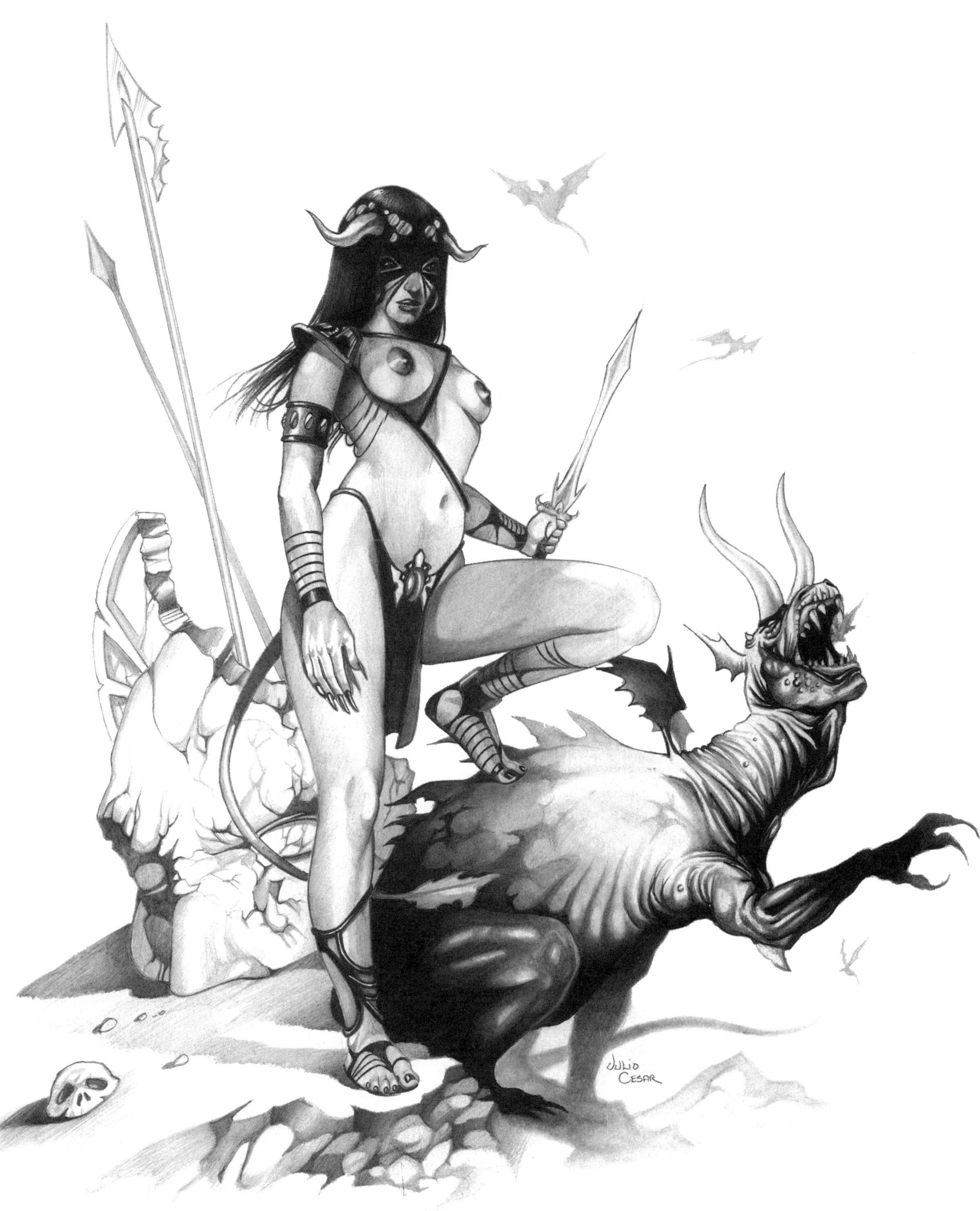

JULIO CESAR

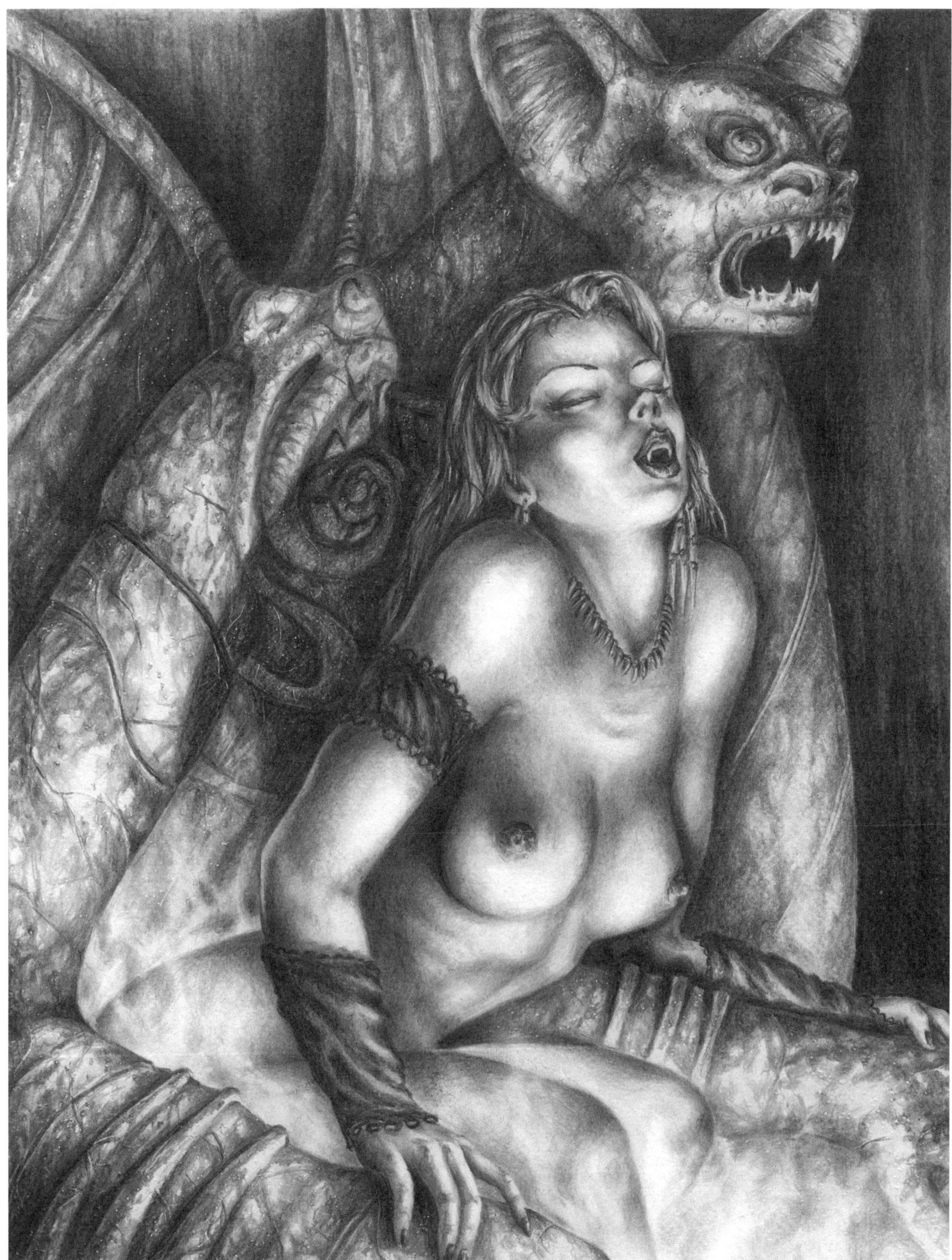

Diego Candia

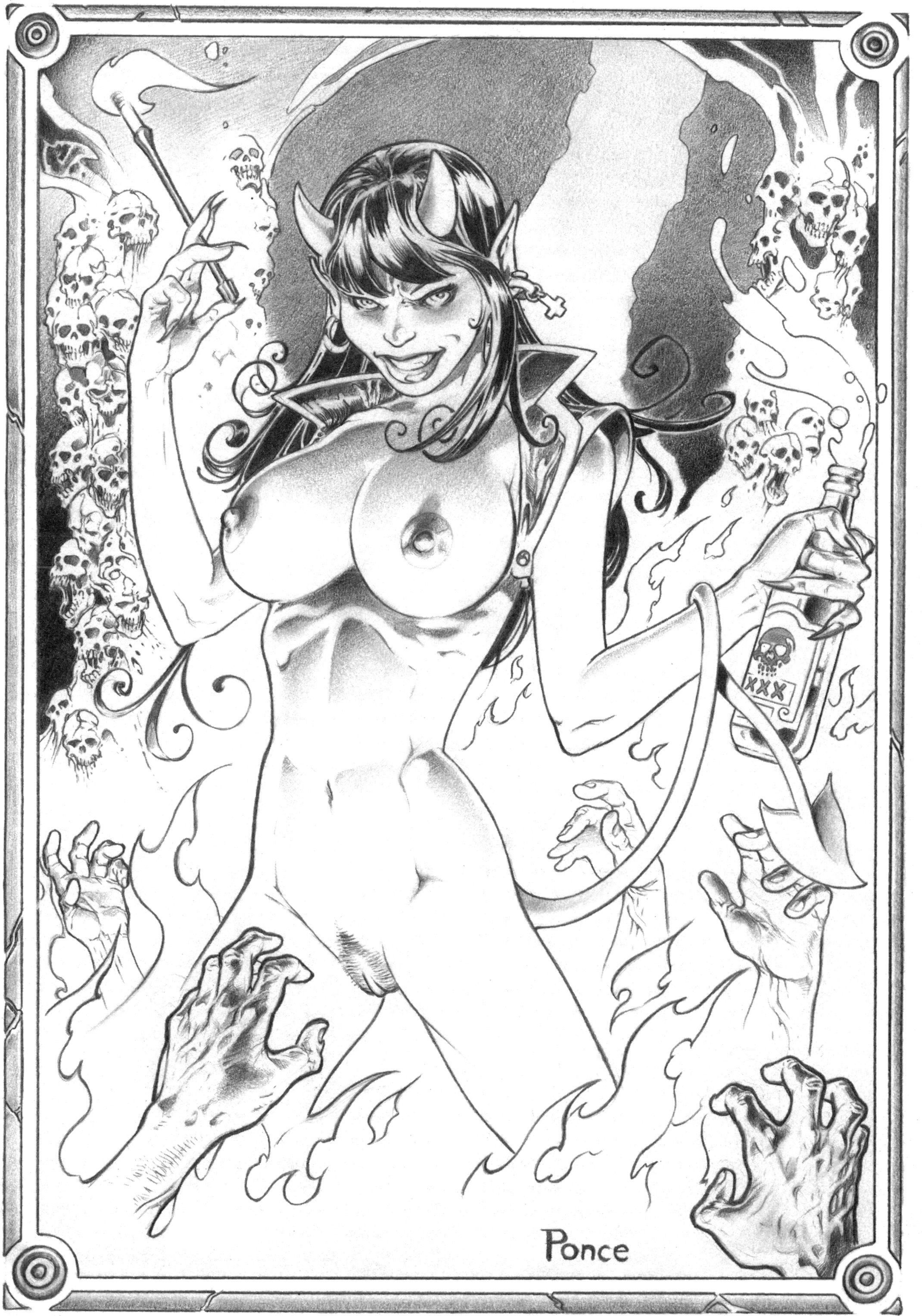

GERMAN PONCE

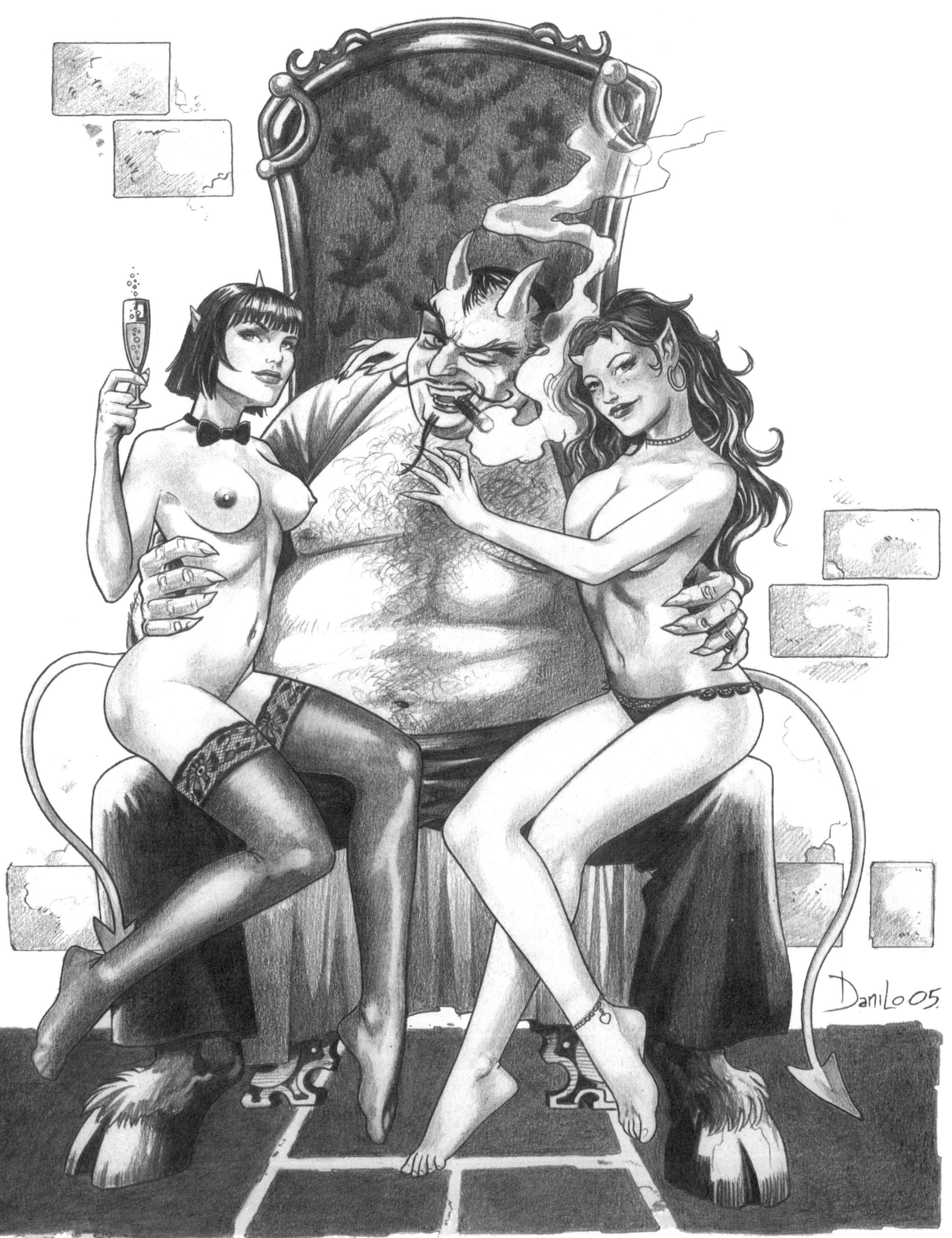

DANILO GUIDA

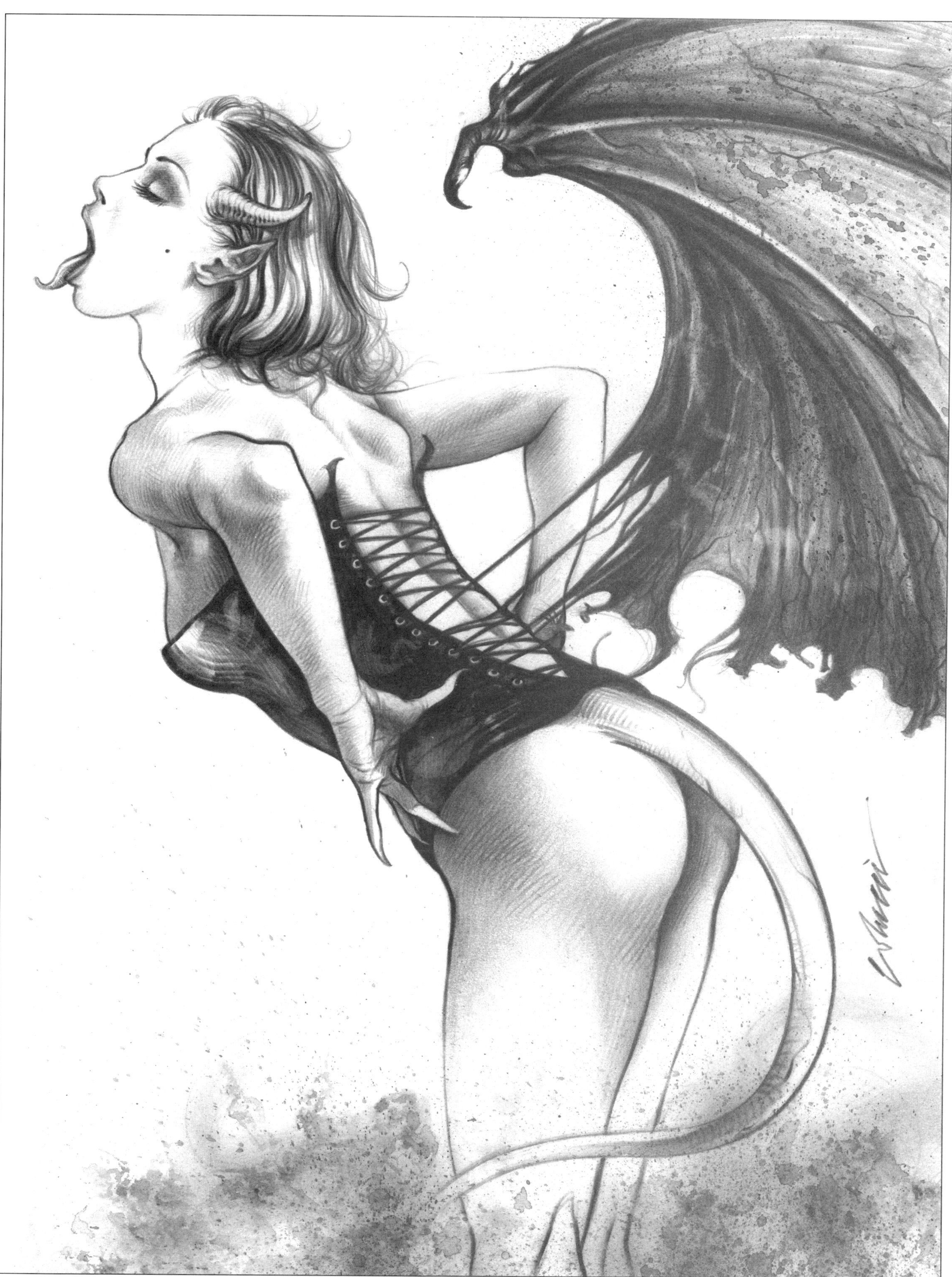

Alejandro Colucci

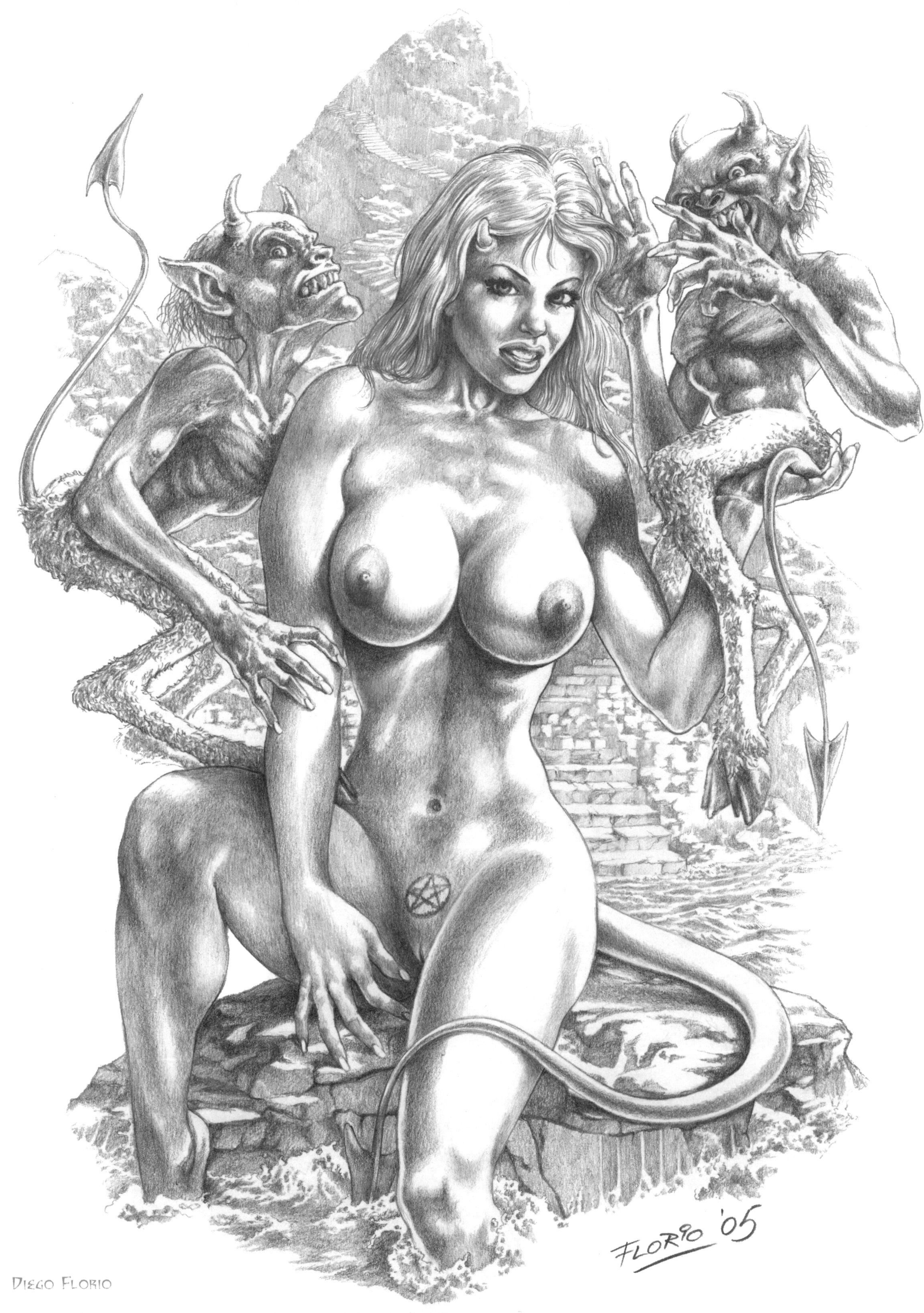

Diego Florio

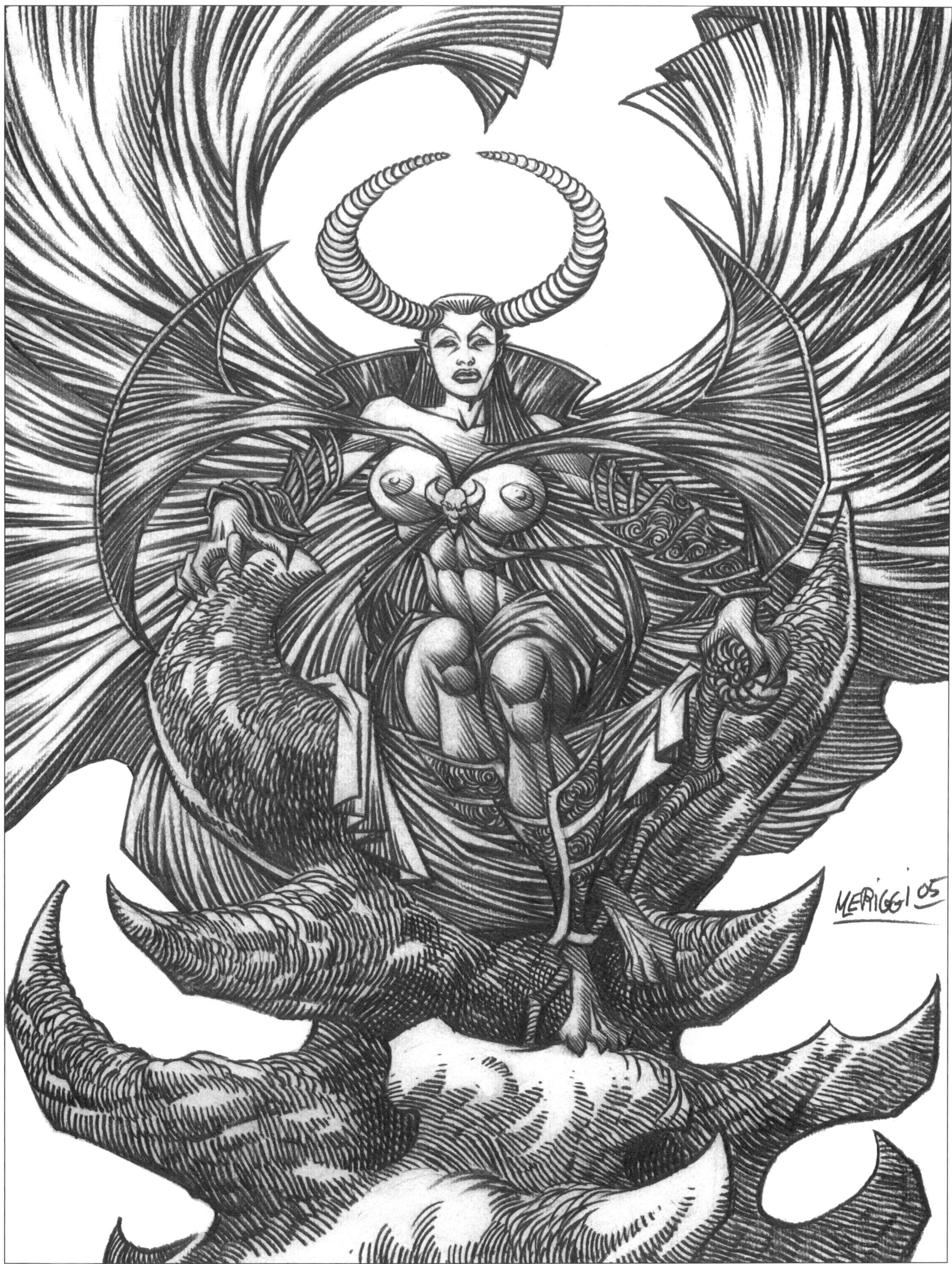

RUBEN MERIGGI

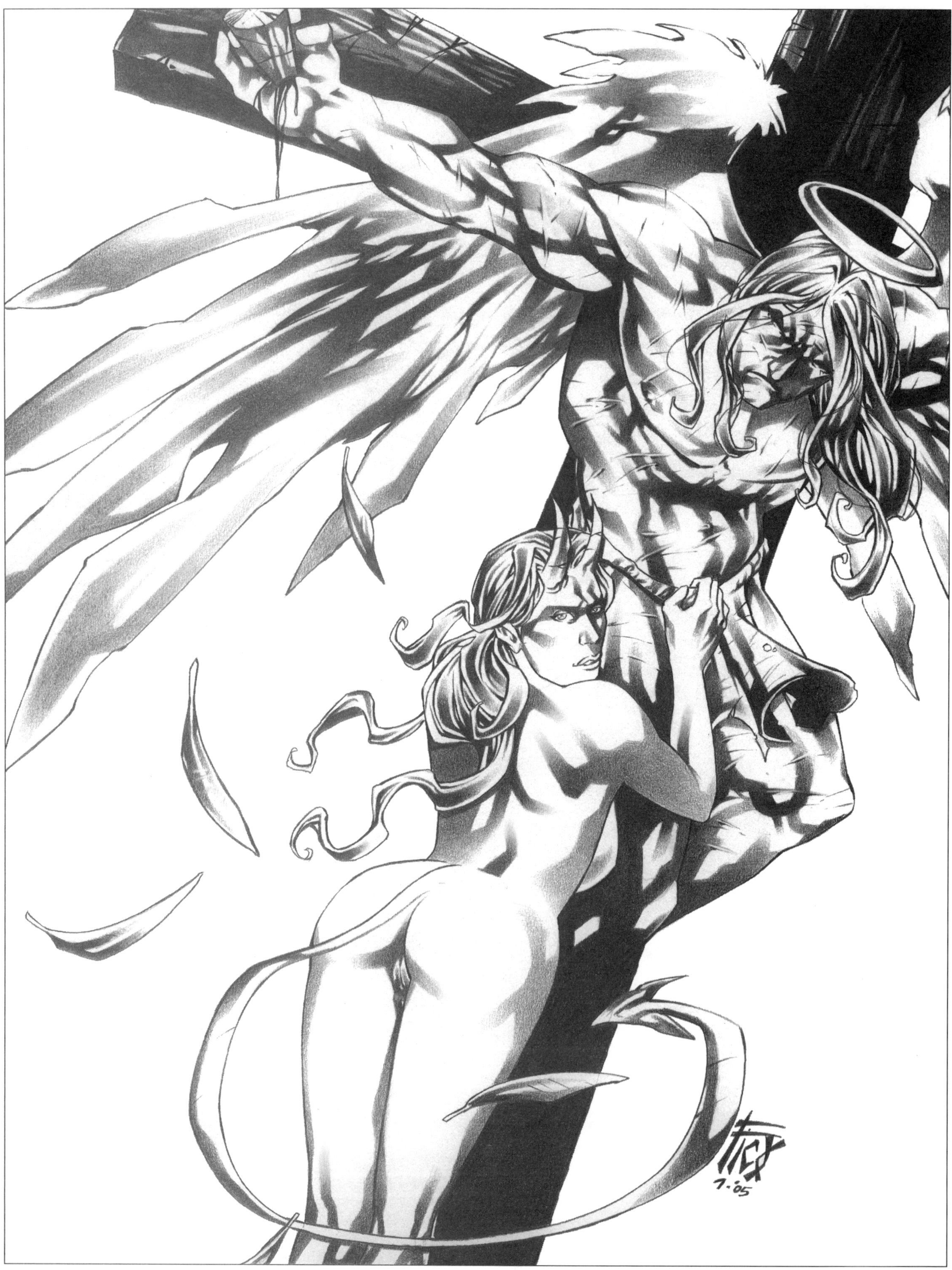

Federico Ossio

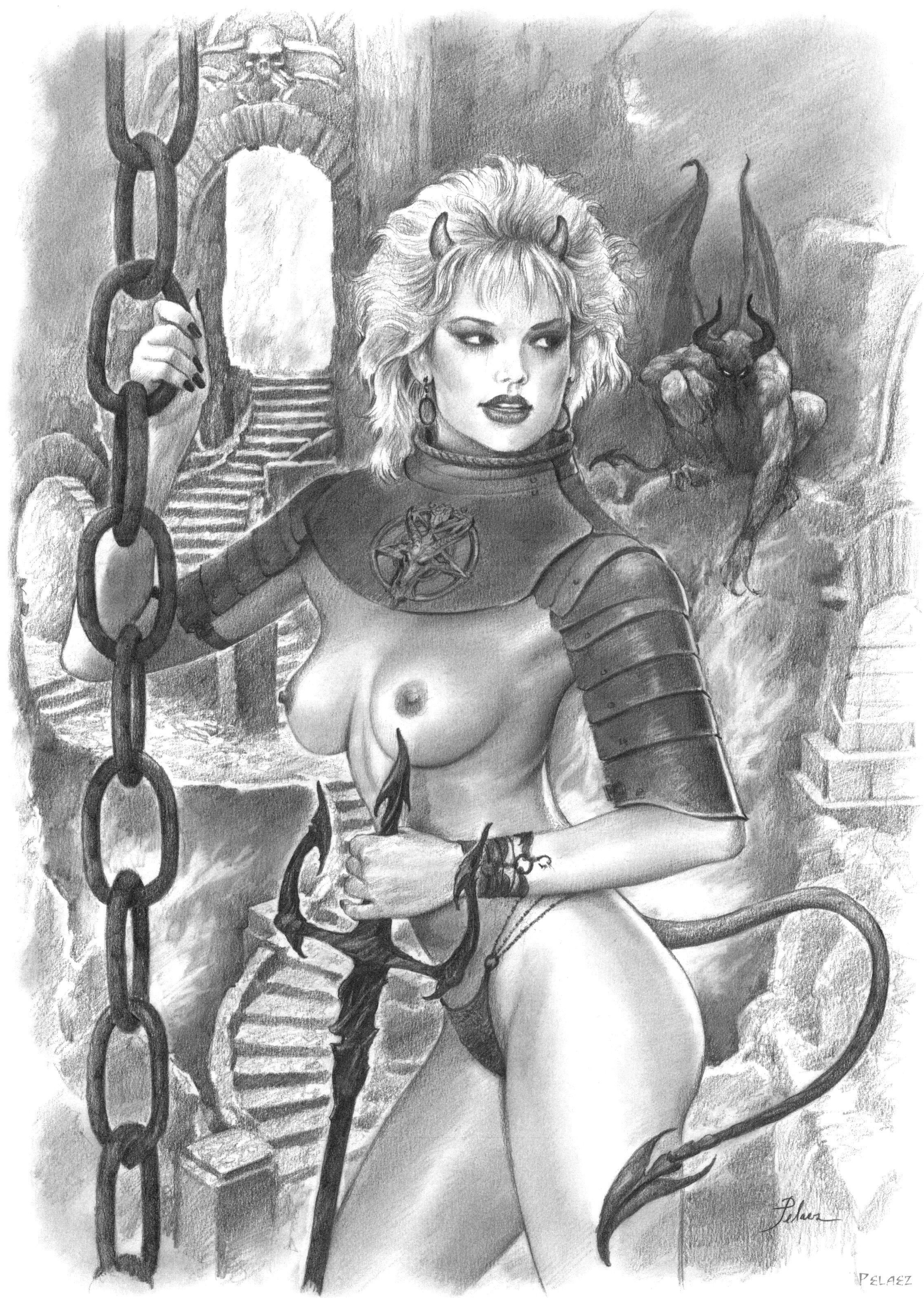

PELAEZ

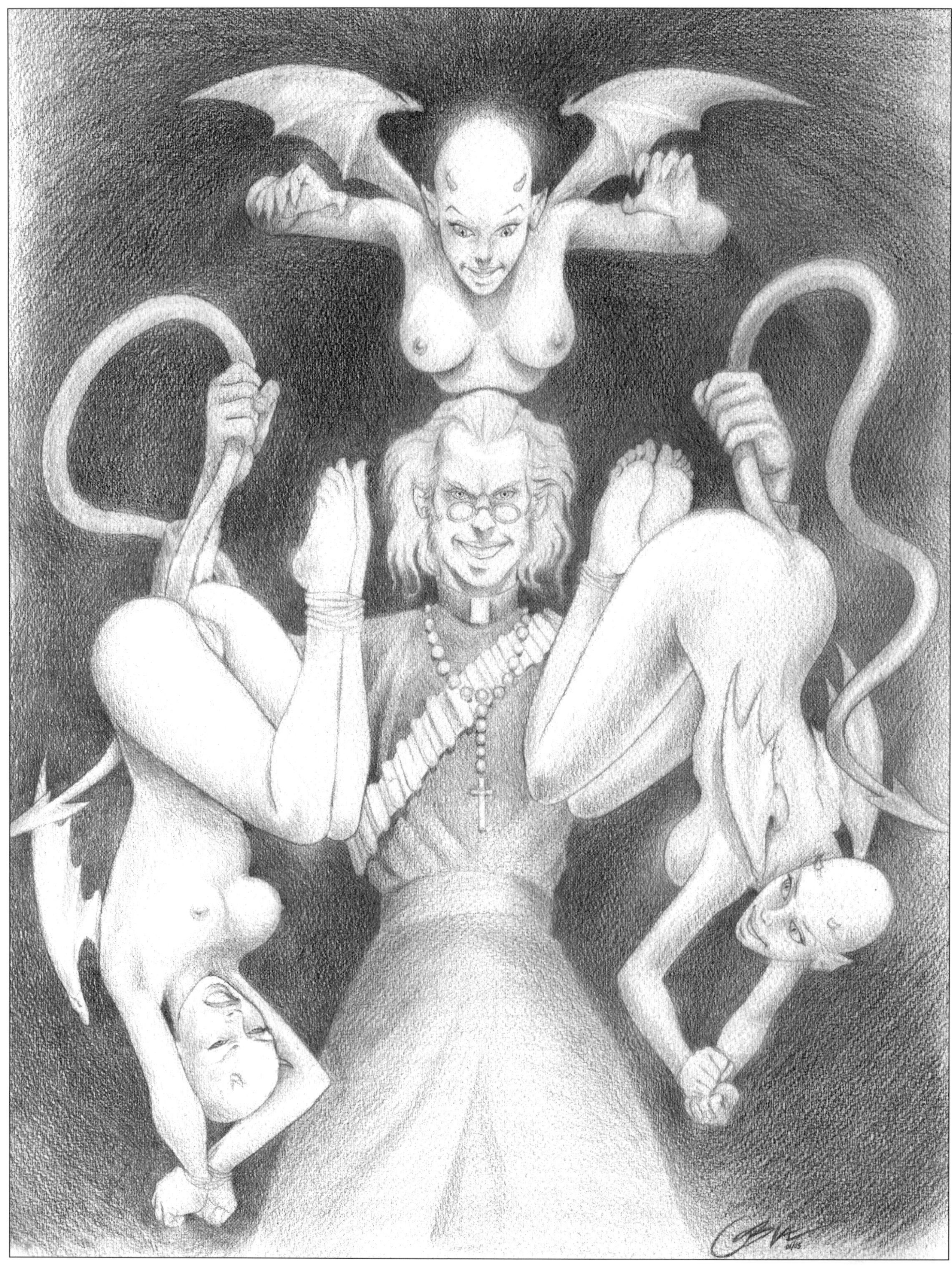

Gabriel Bobillo

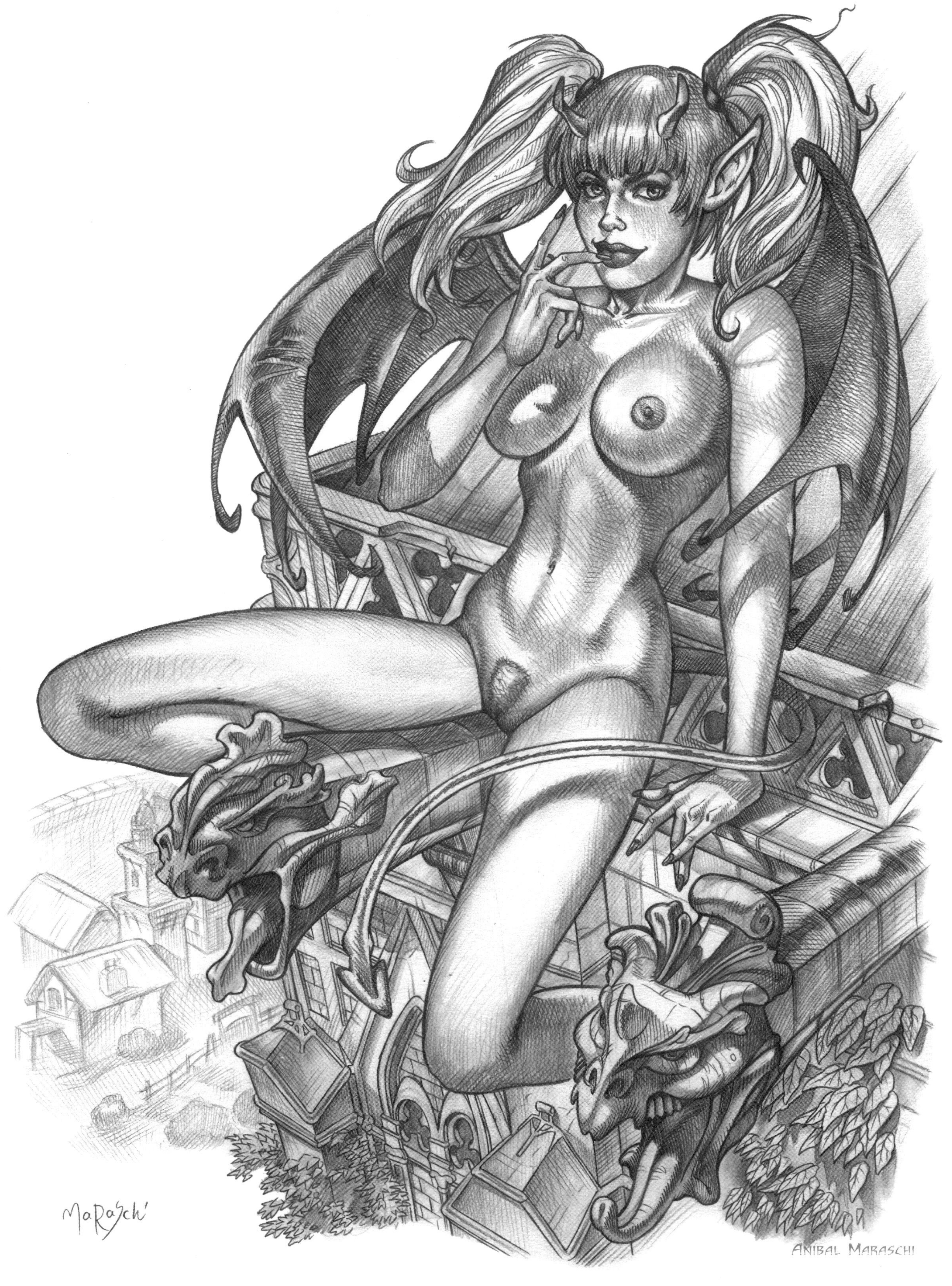
Maraschi
ANIBAL MARASCHI

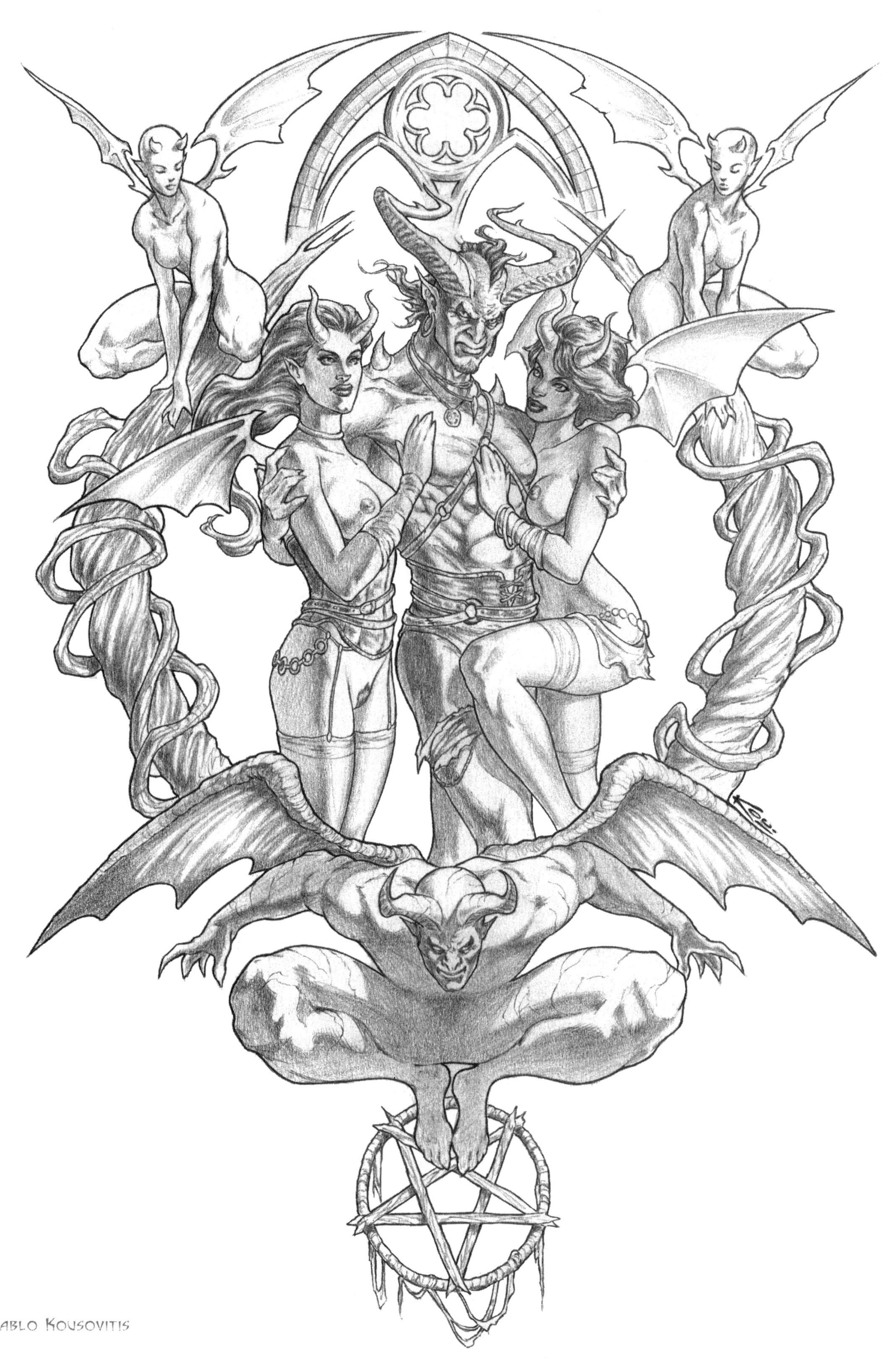

Pablo Kousovitis

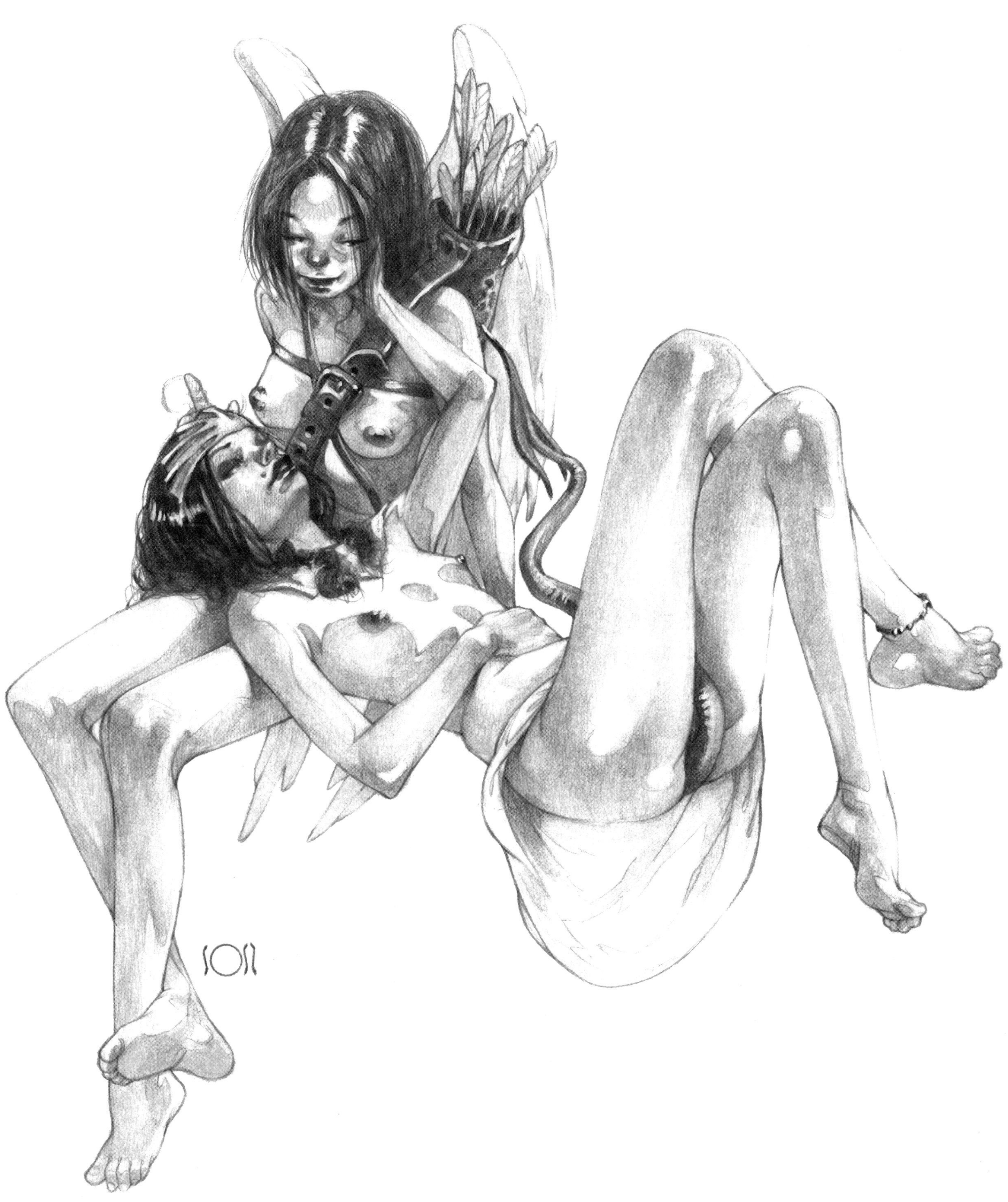

MARCELO SOSA

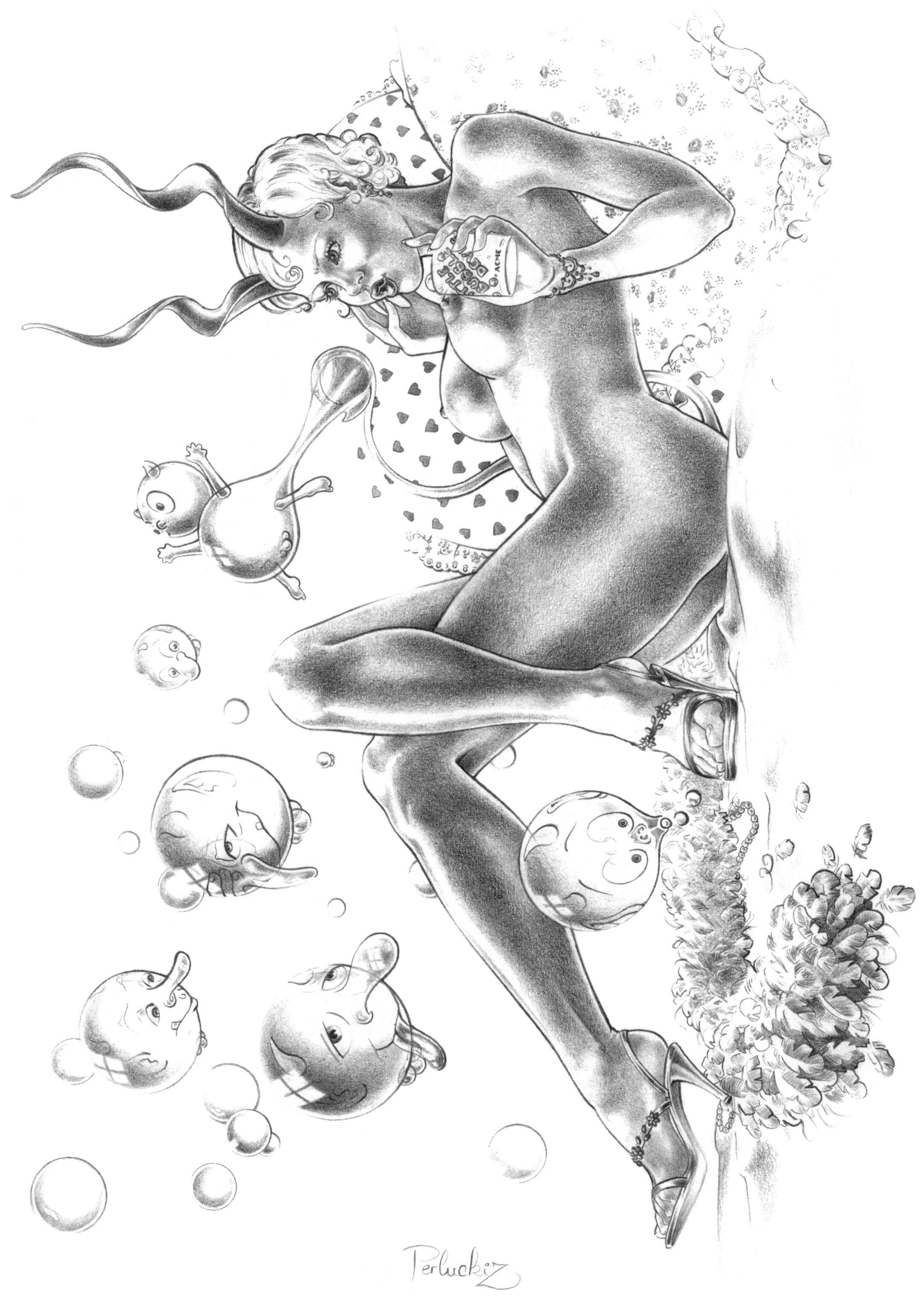

PERLA PERLUCKY

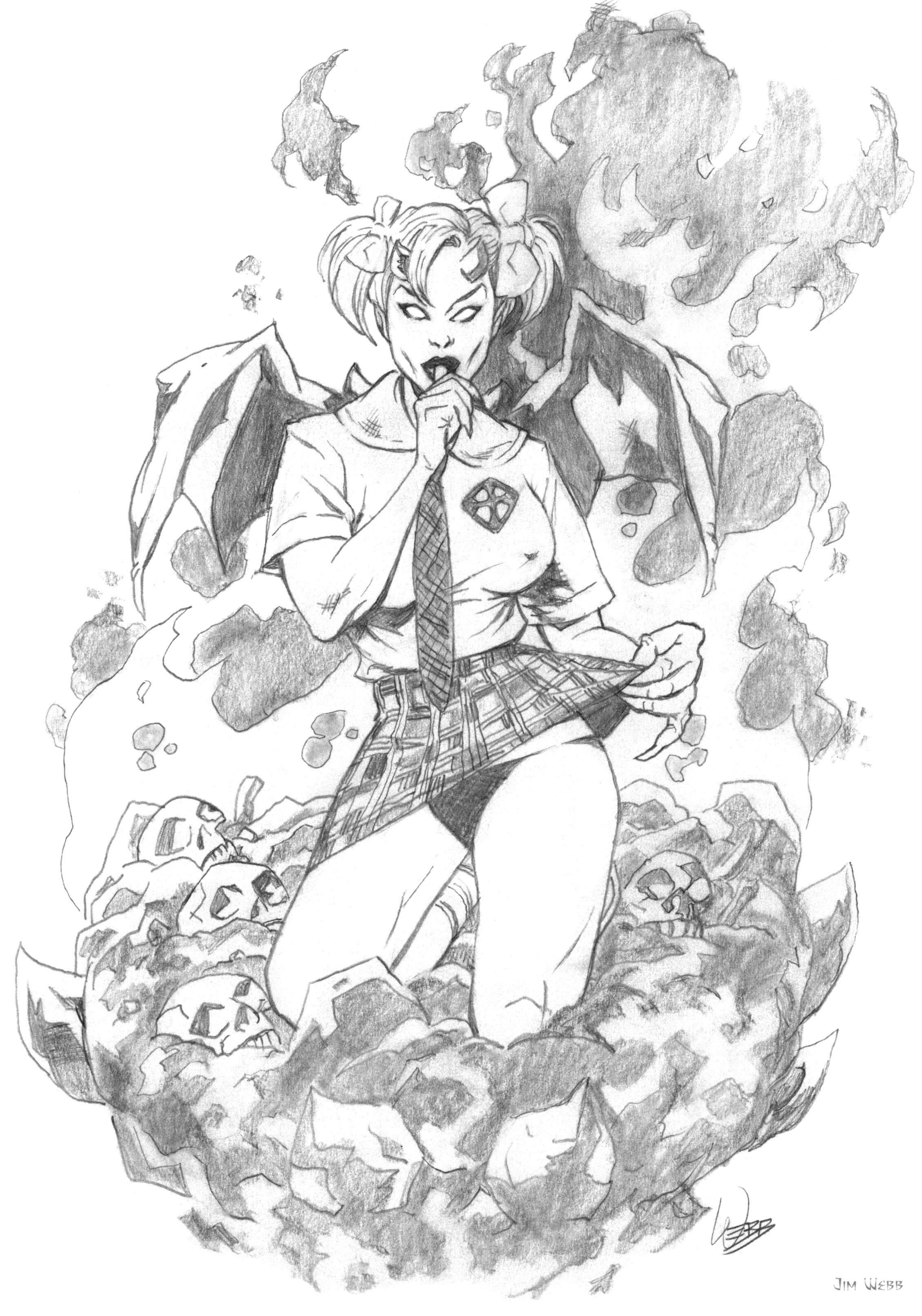

Jim Webb

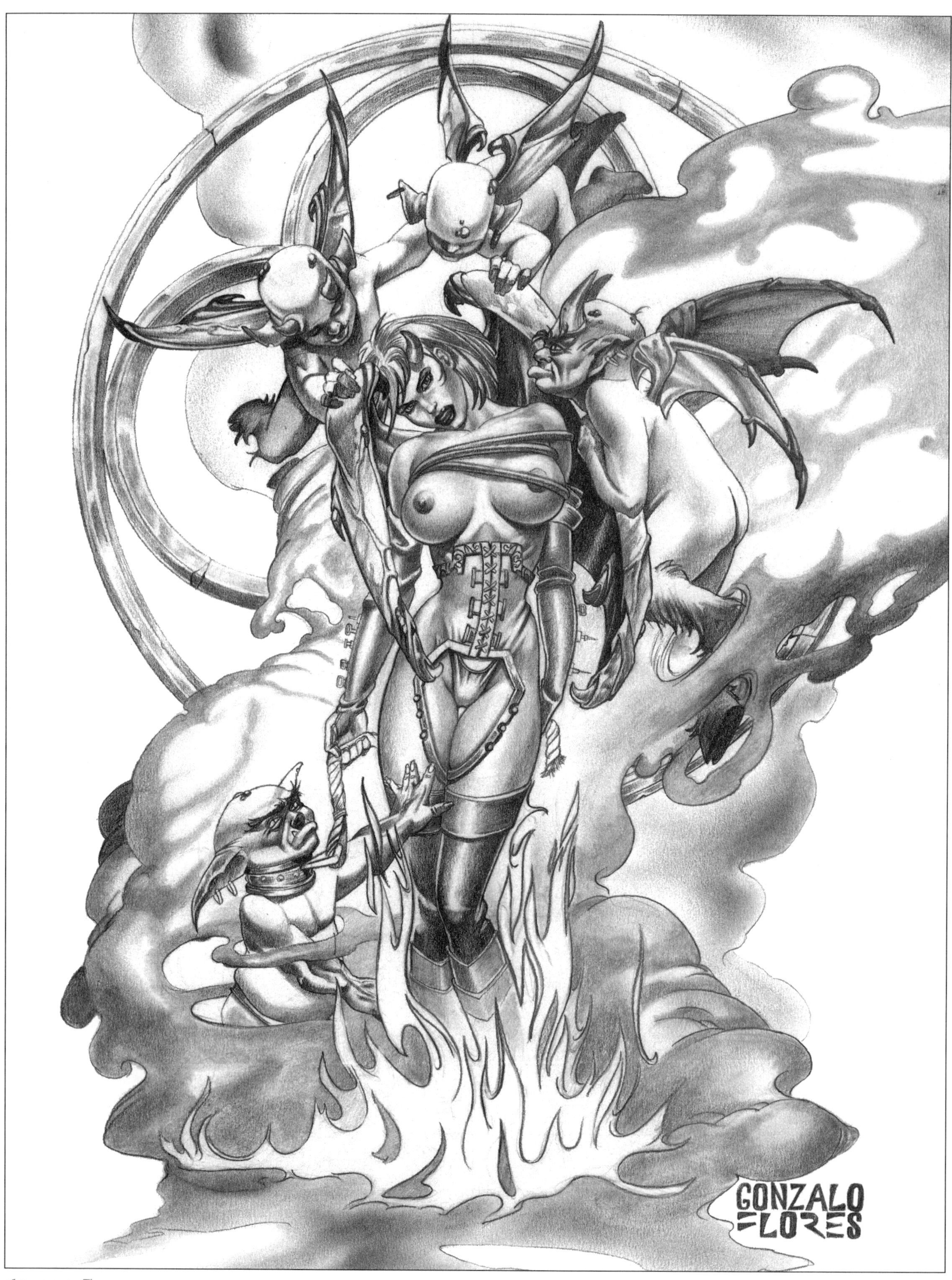

GONZALO FLORES

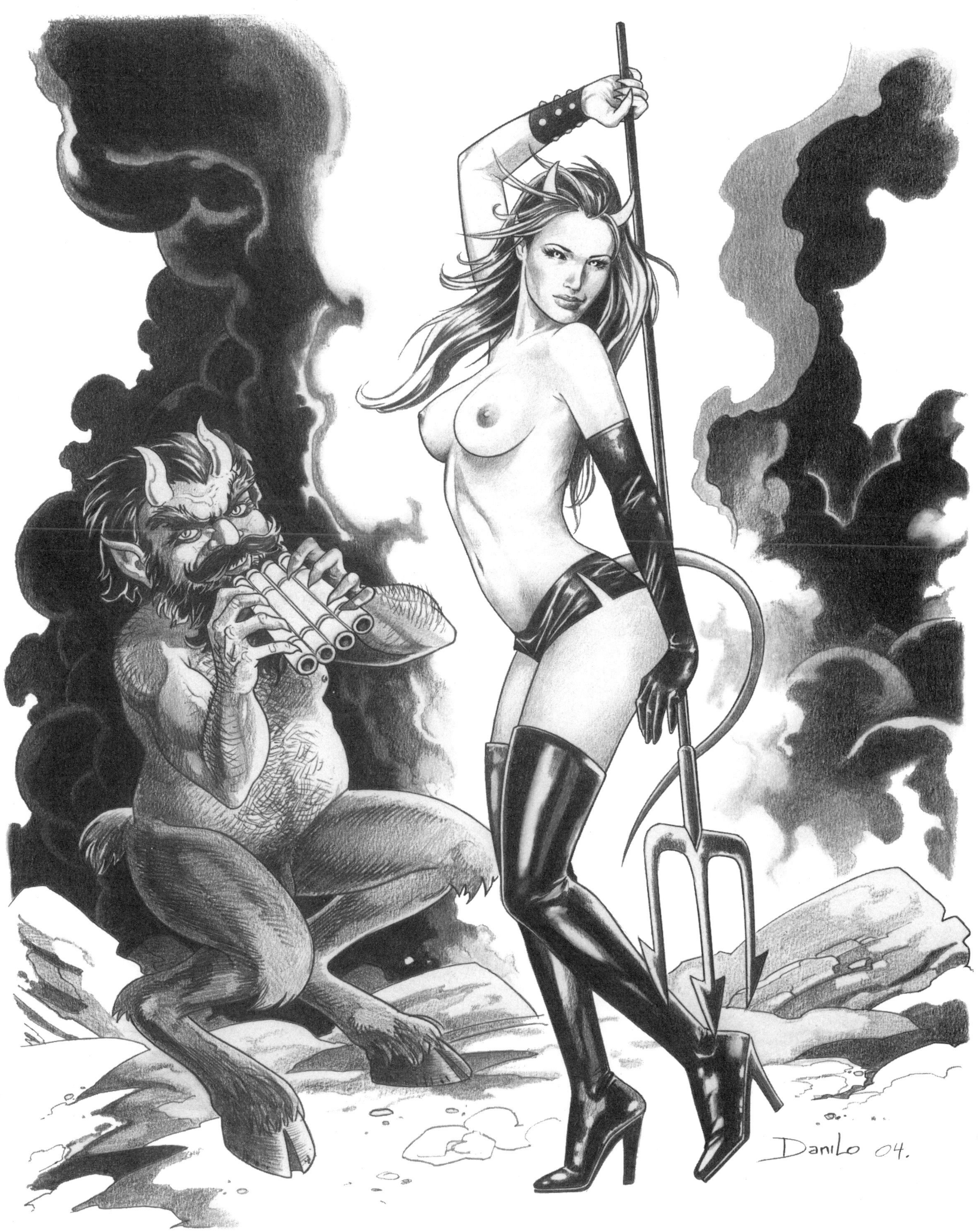

Danilo Guida

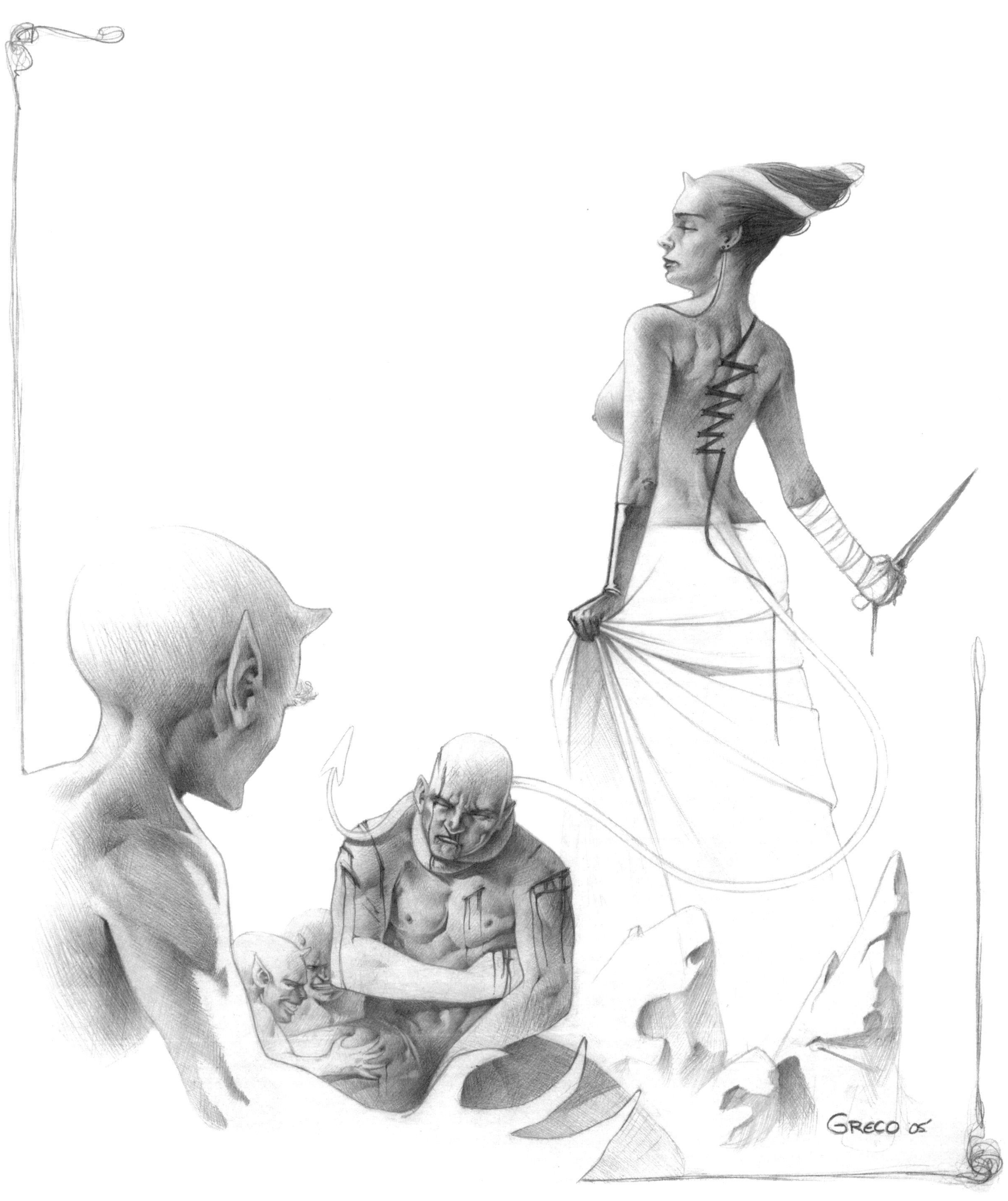

DIEGO GRECO

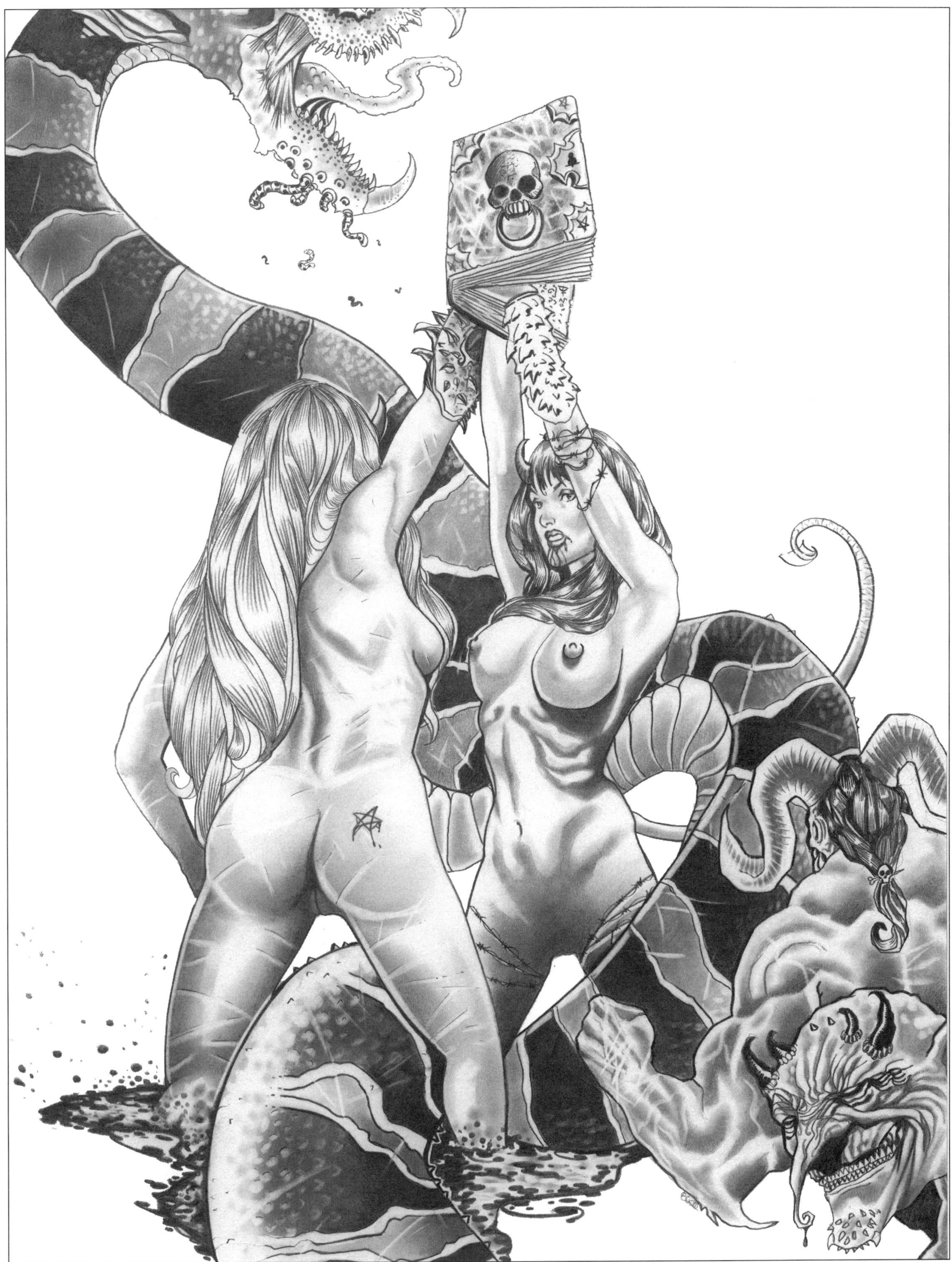
BUCI

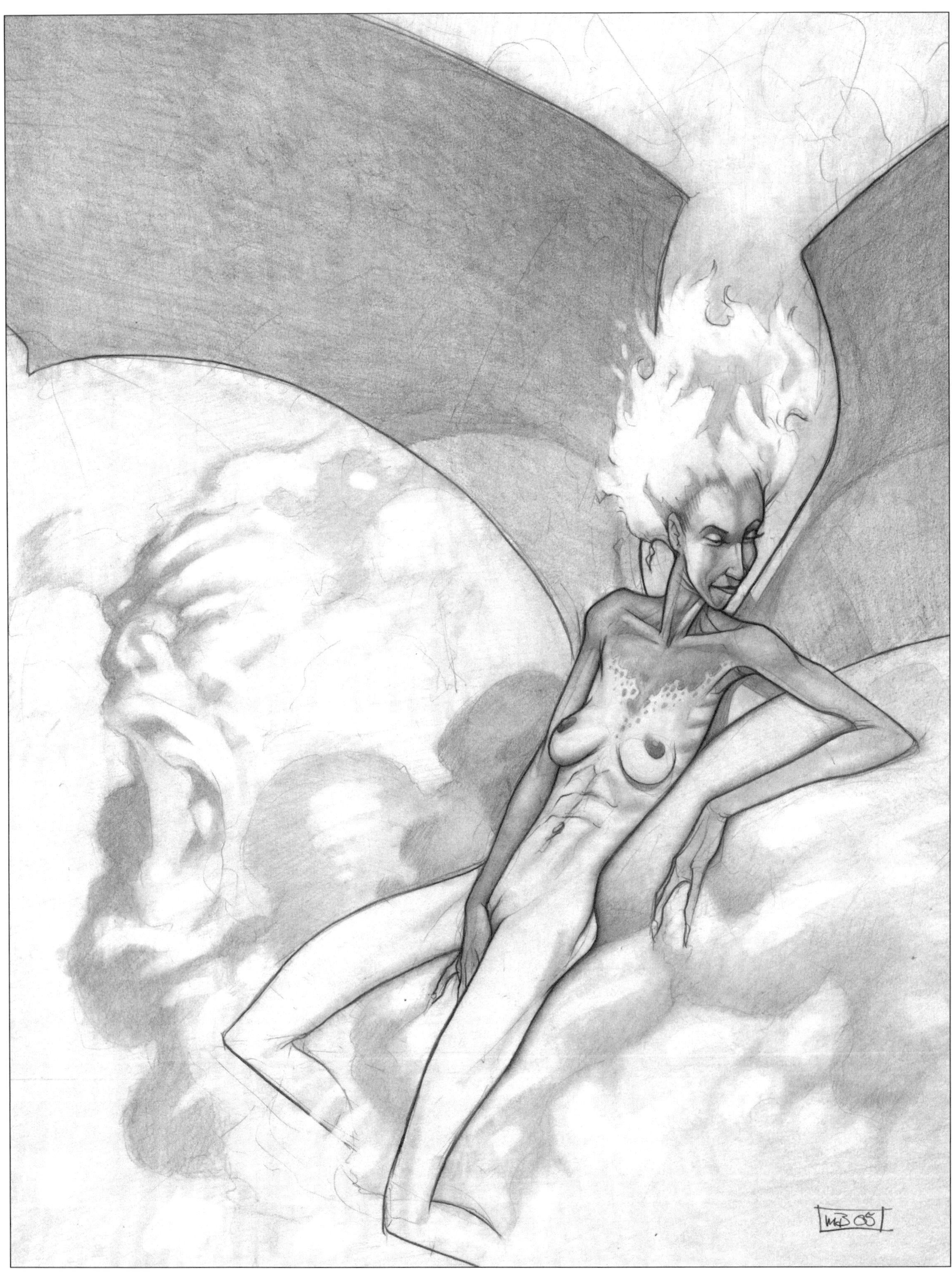

Mitch Byrd

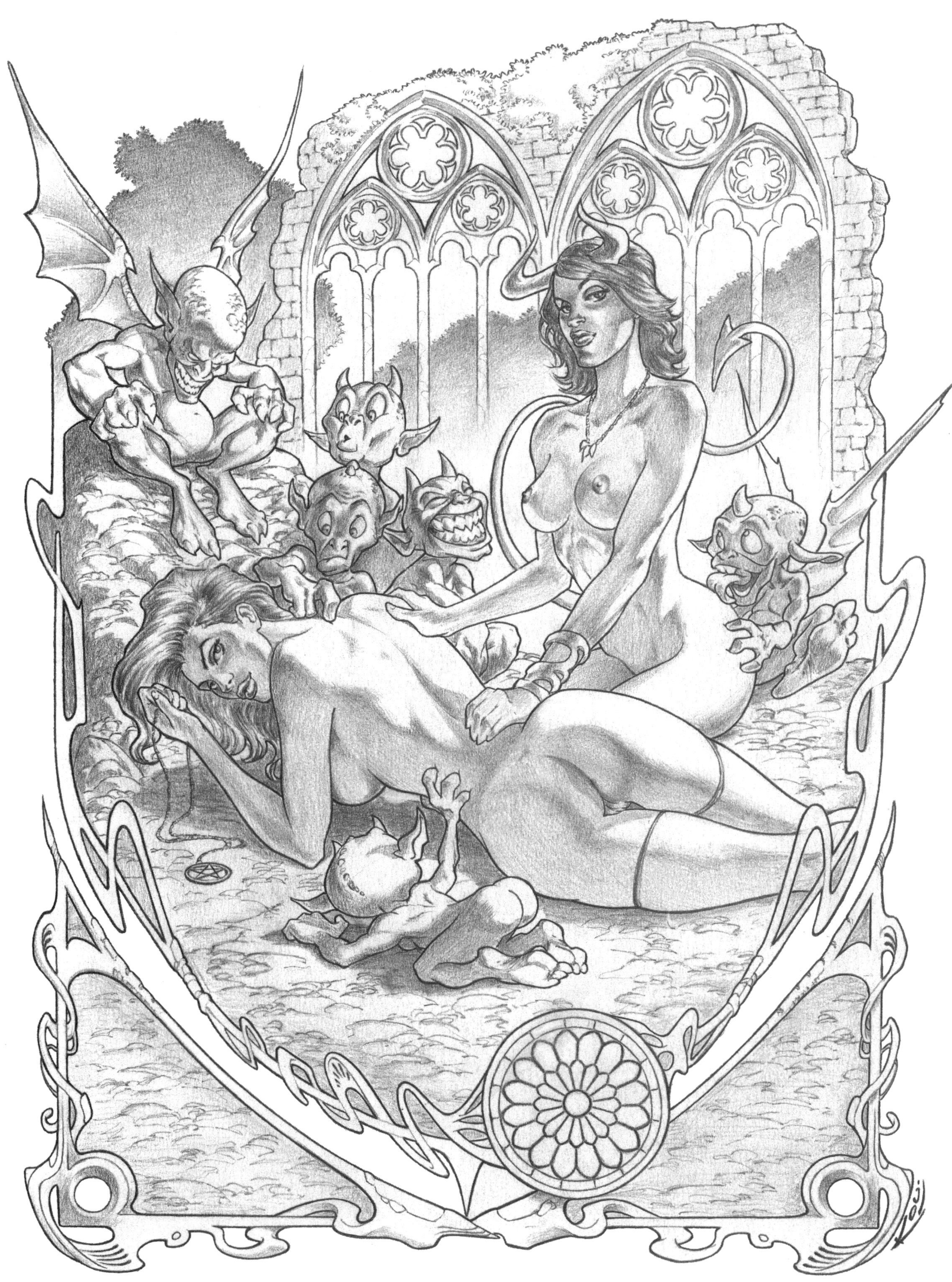

Pablo Kousovitis

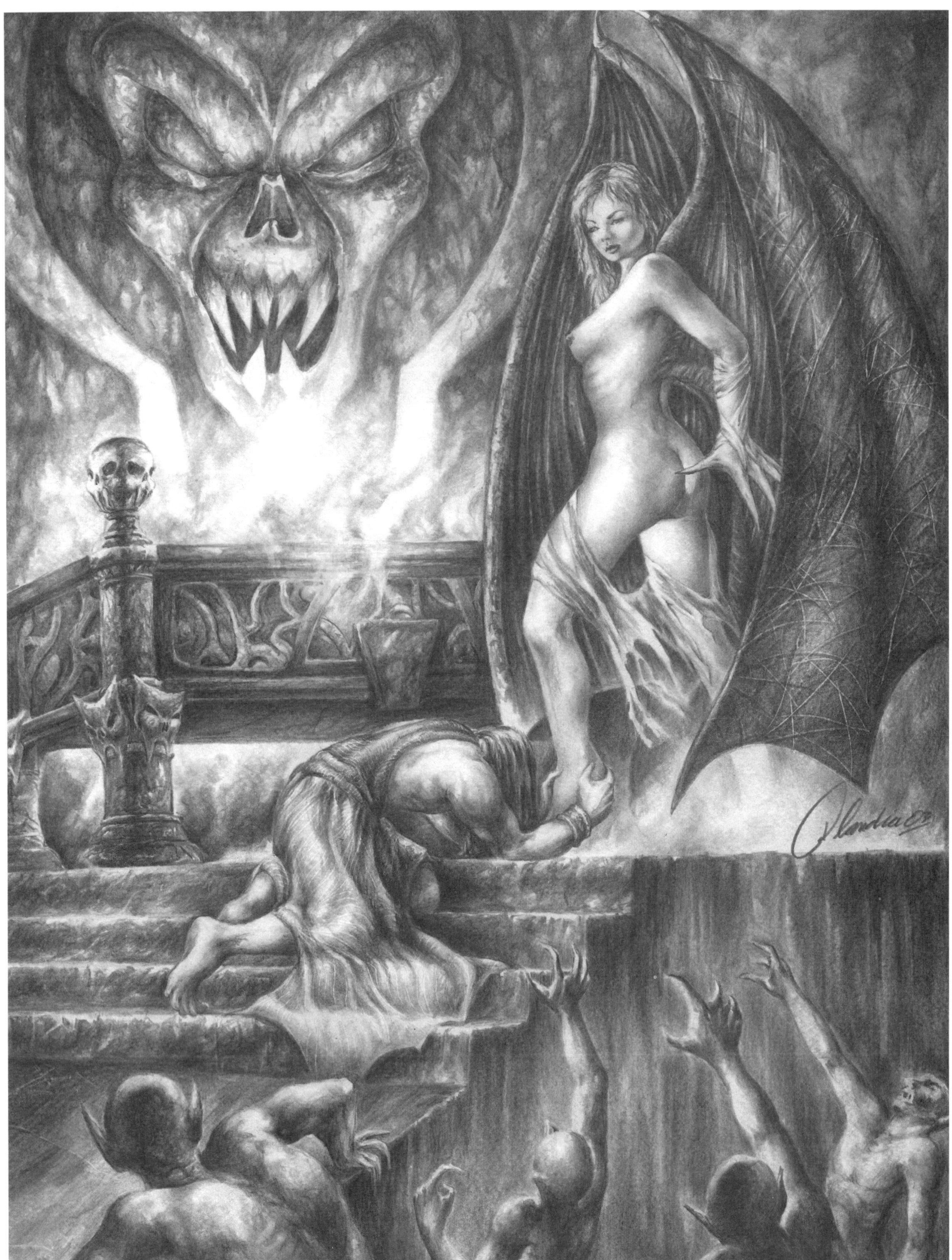

Diego Candia

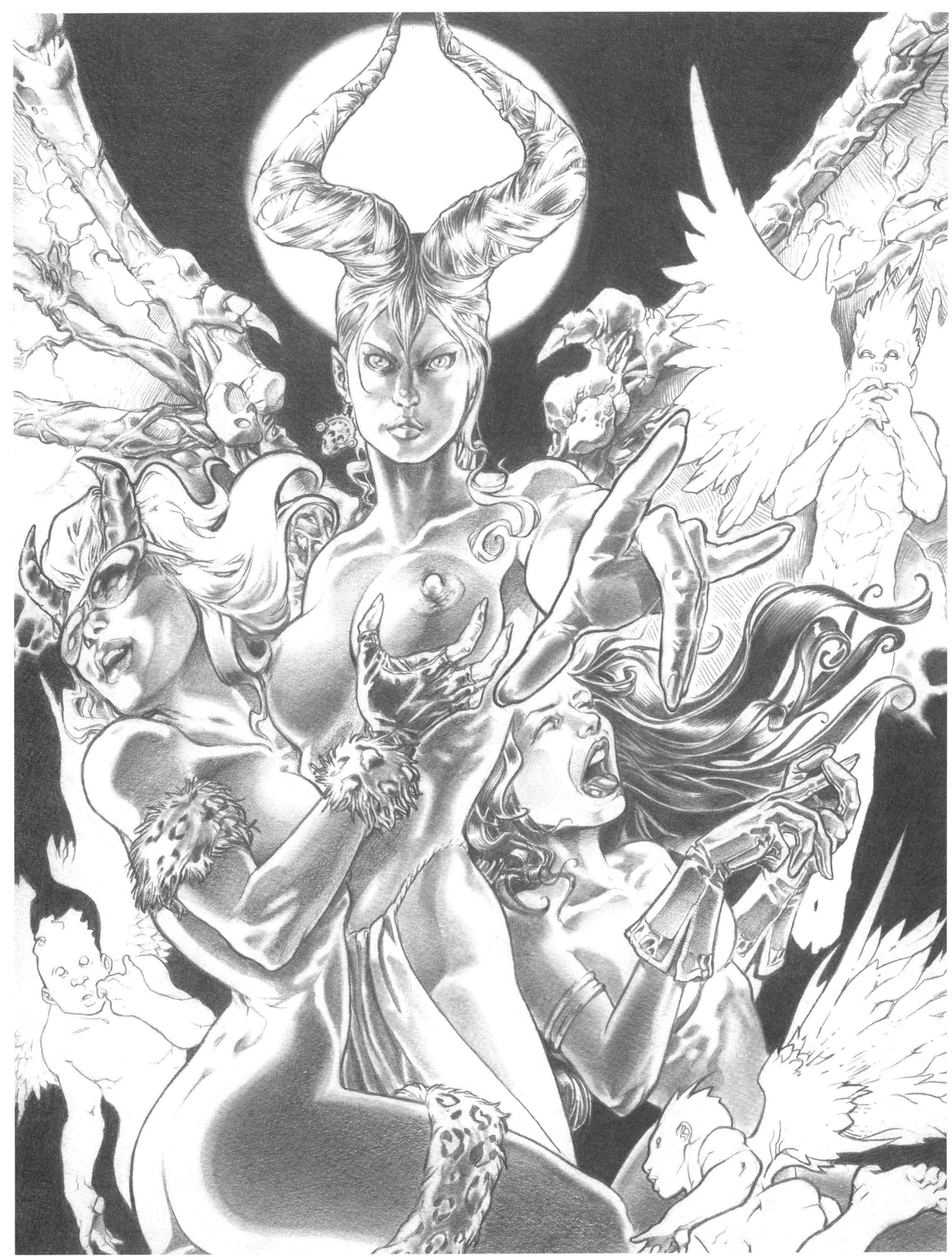

German Ponce

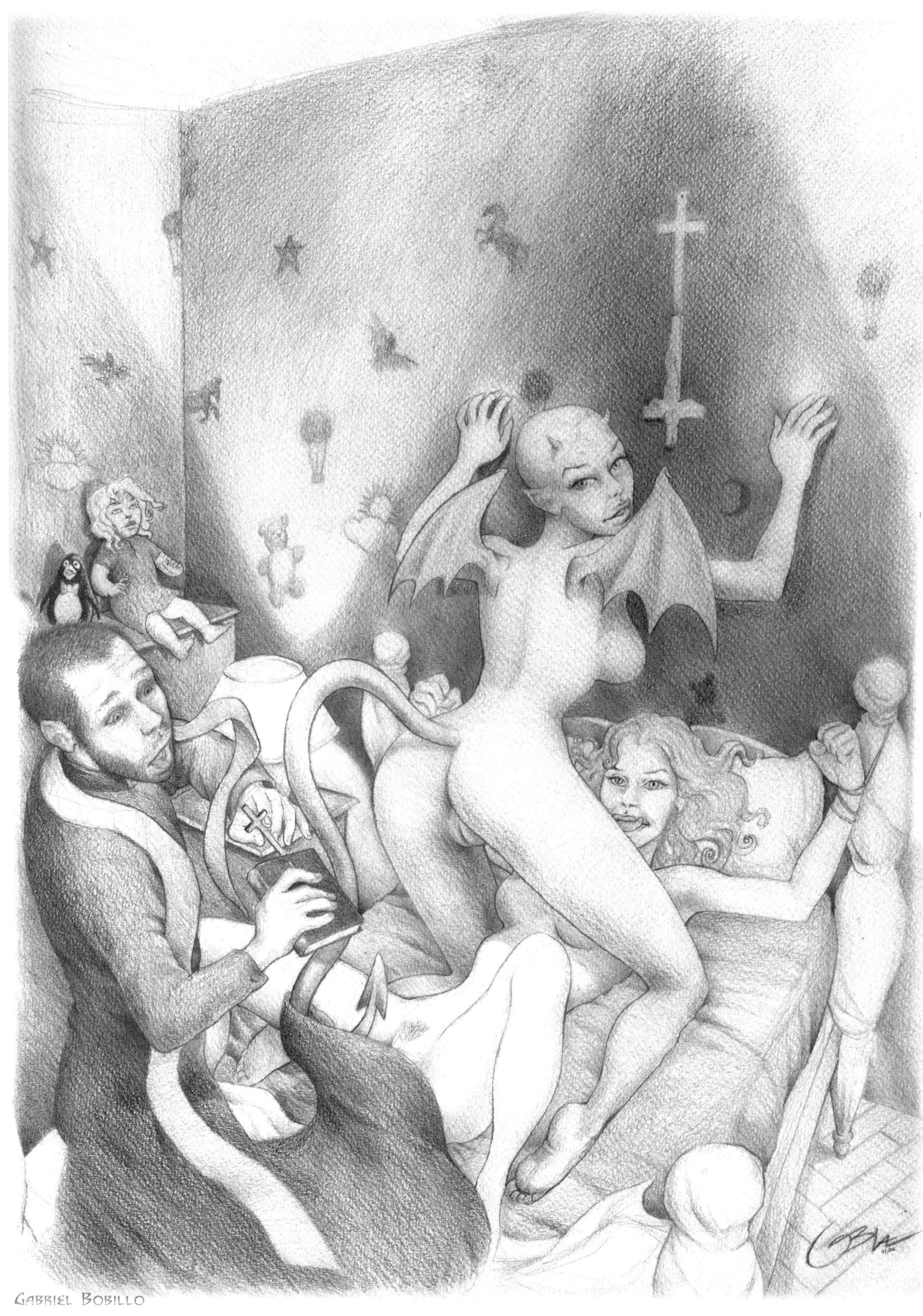

Gabriel Bobillo

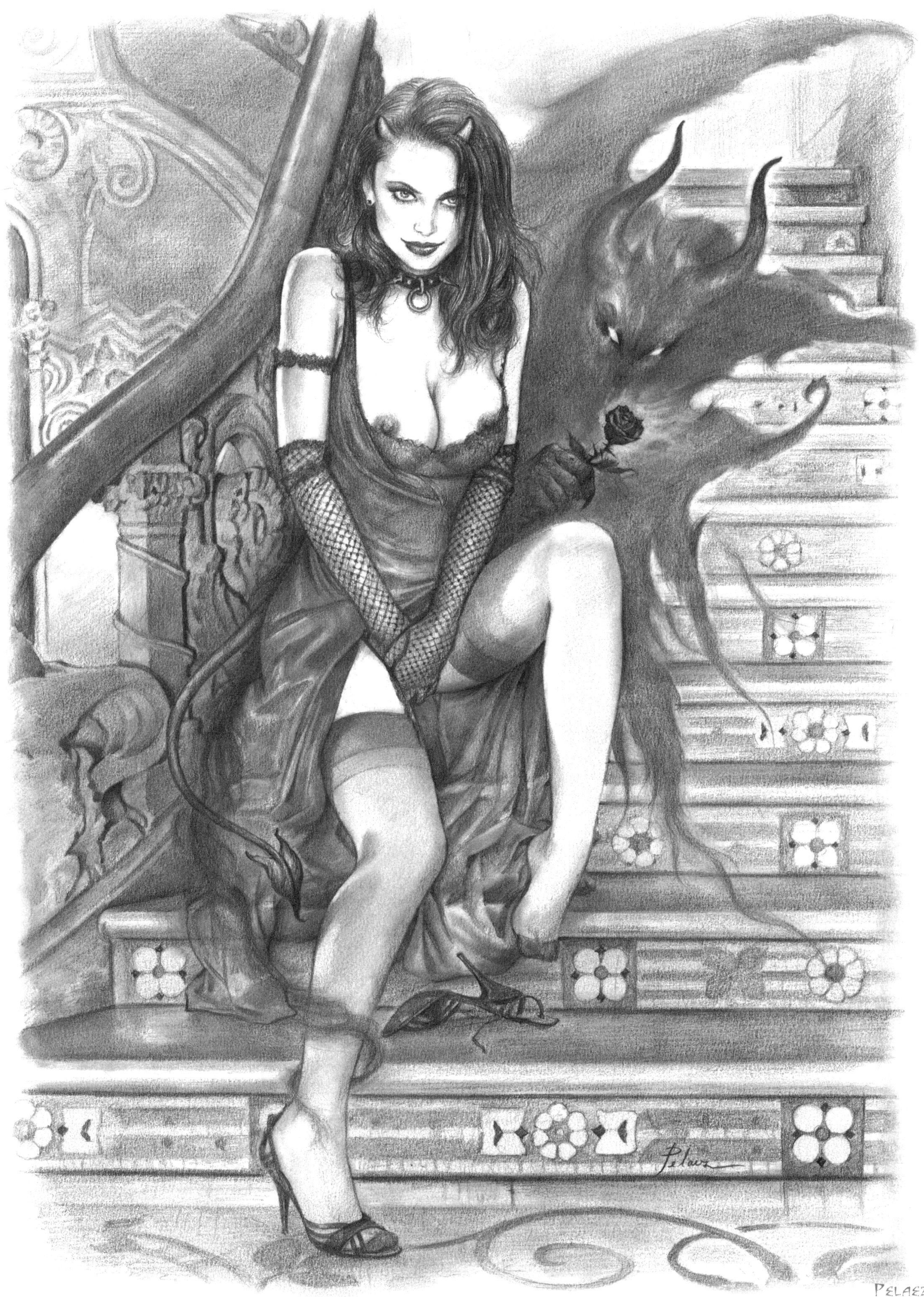

PELAEZ

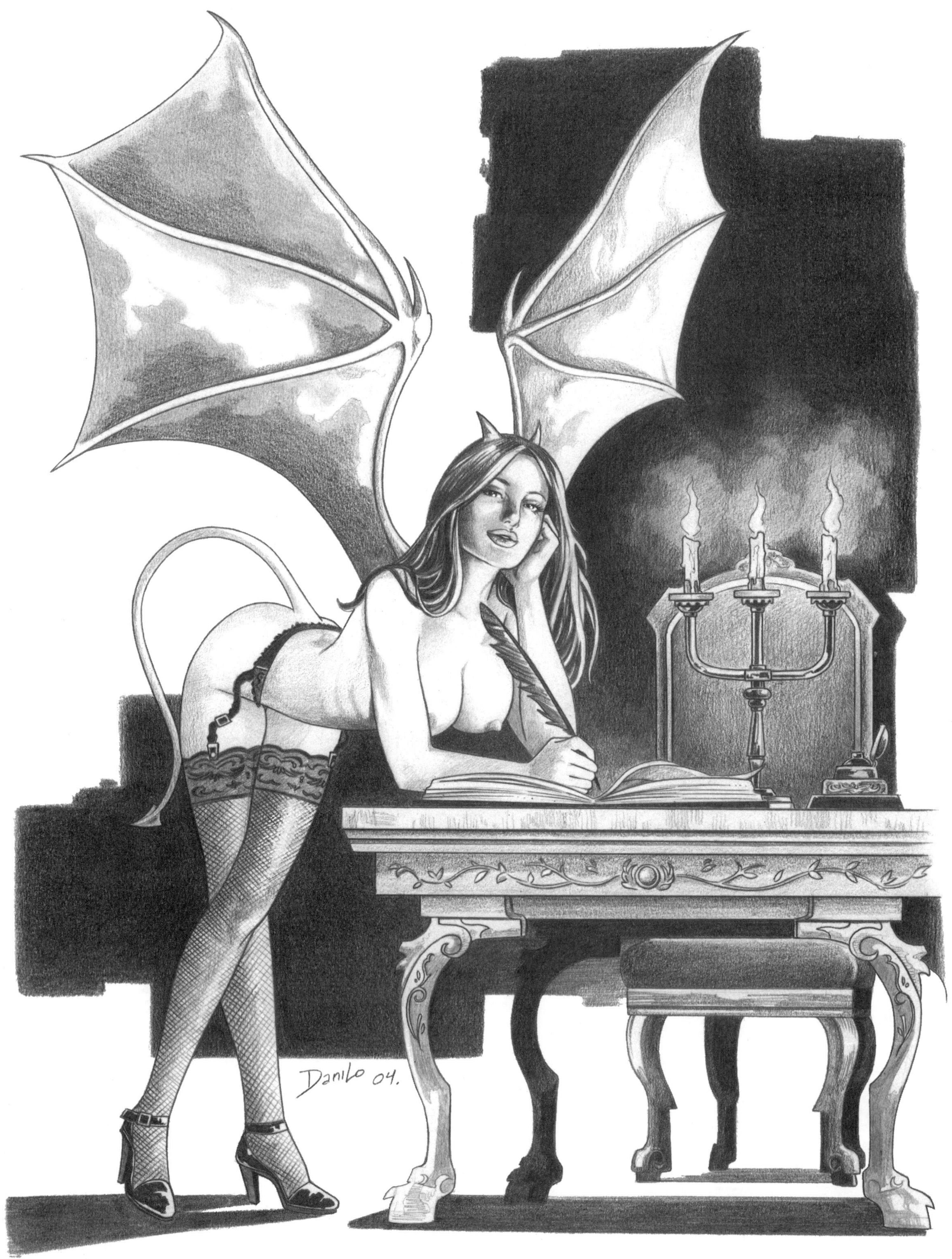

DANILO GUIDA

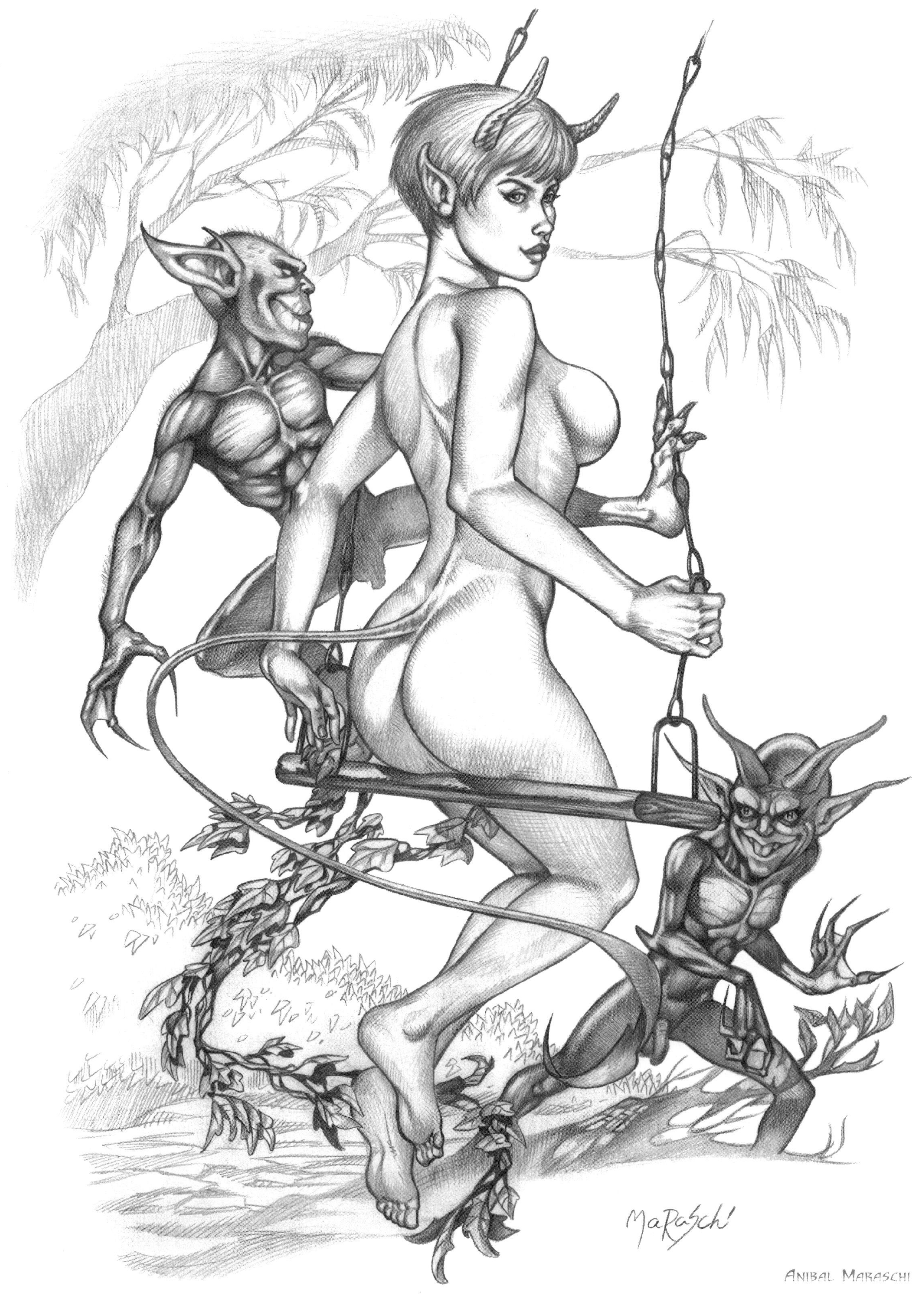

ANIBAL MARASCHI

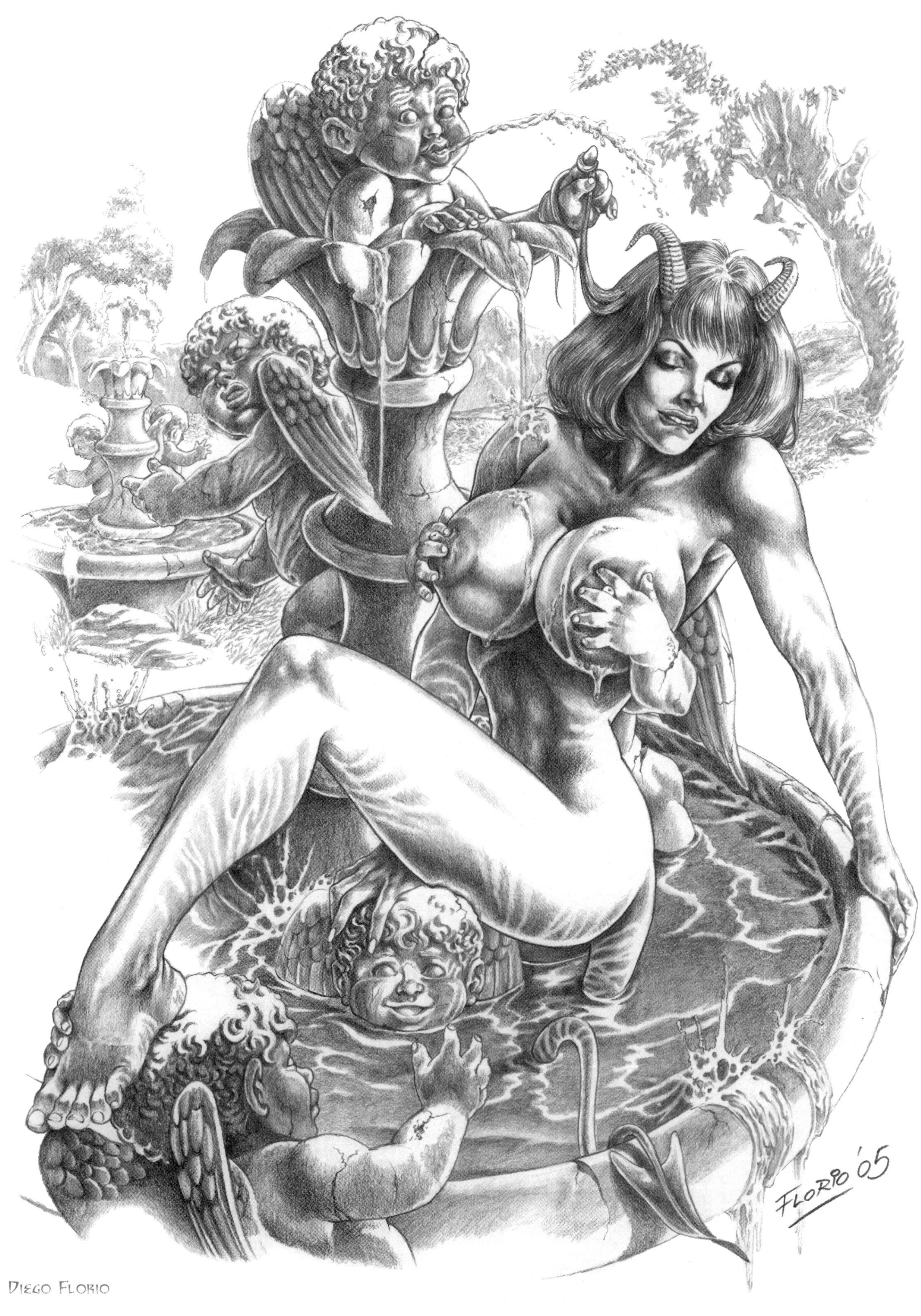

DIEGO FLORIO

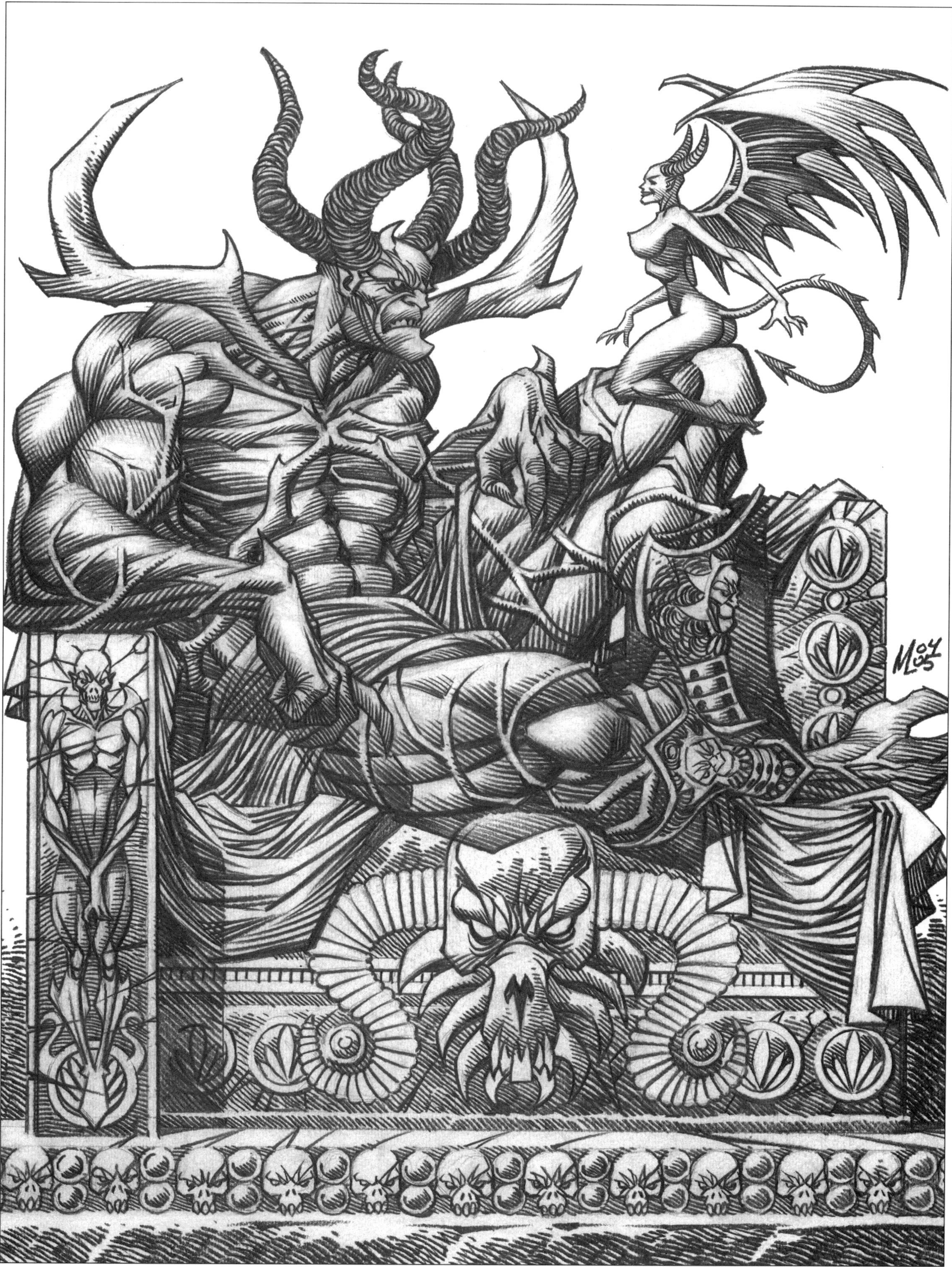

Ruben Meriggi

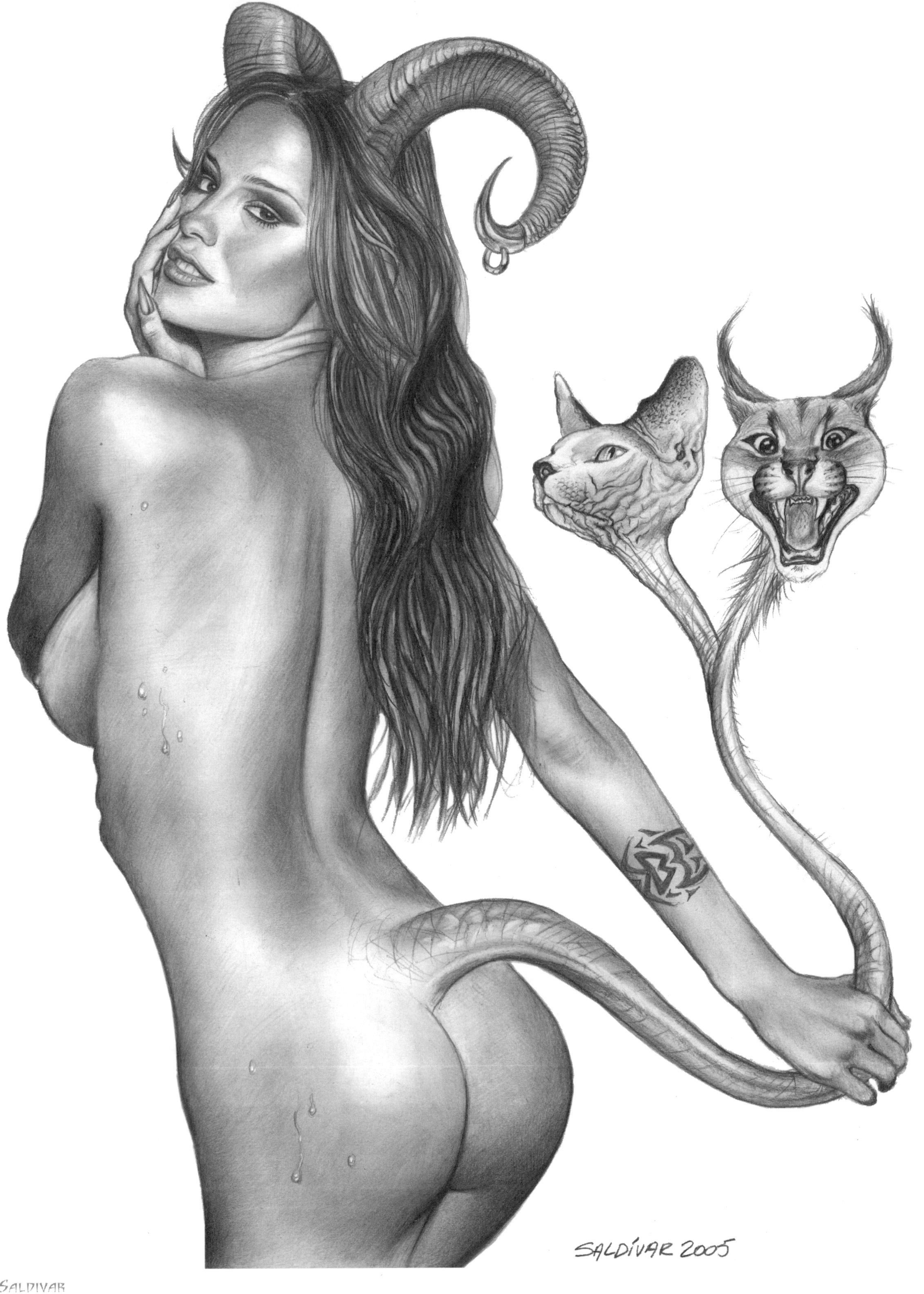
SALDÍVAR 2005

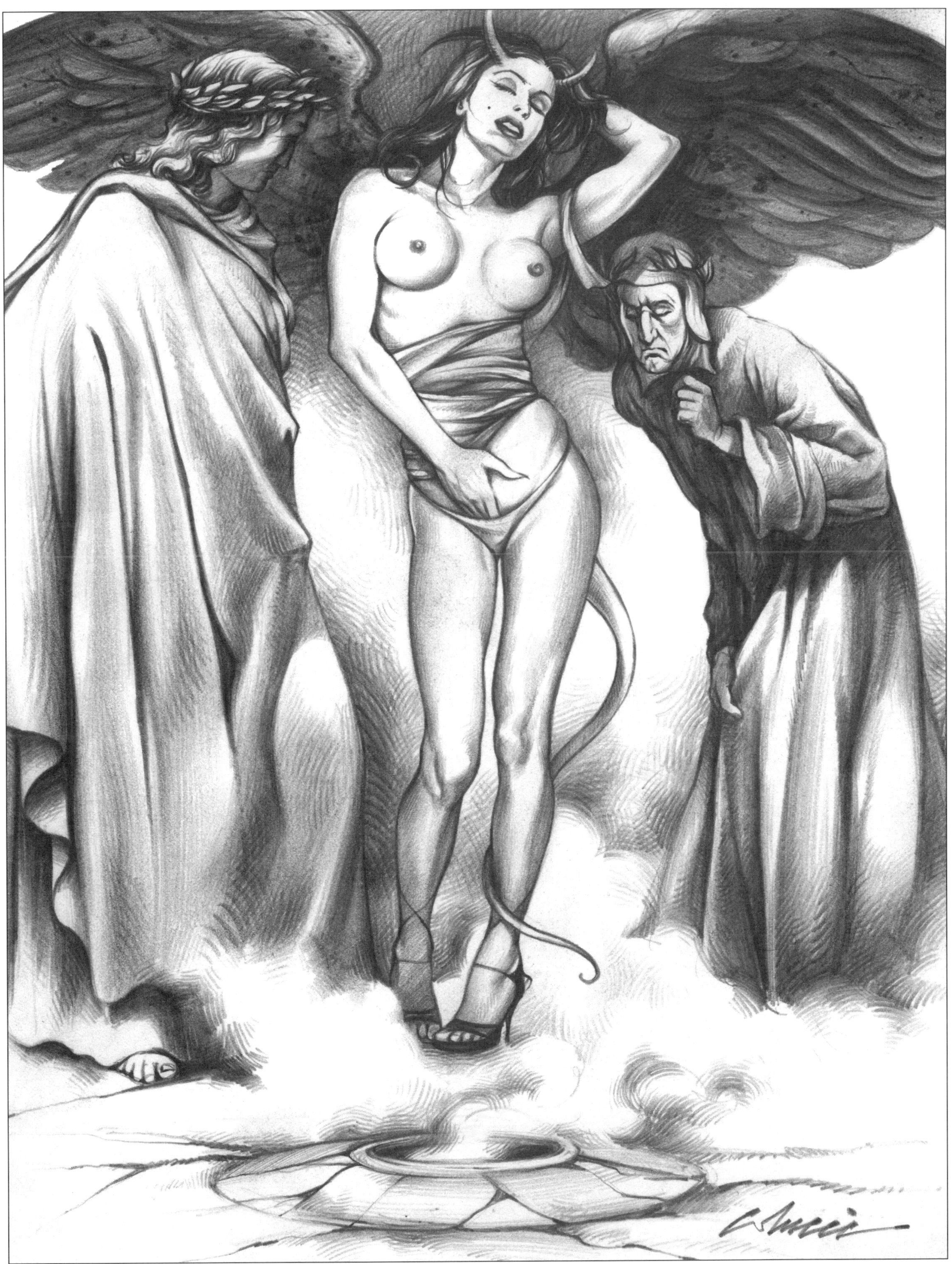

Alejandro Colucci

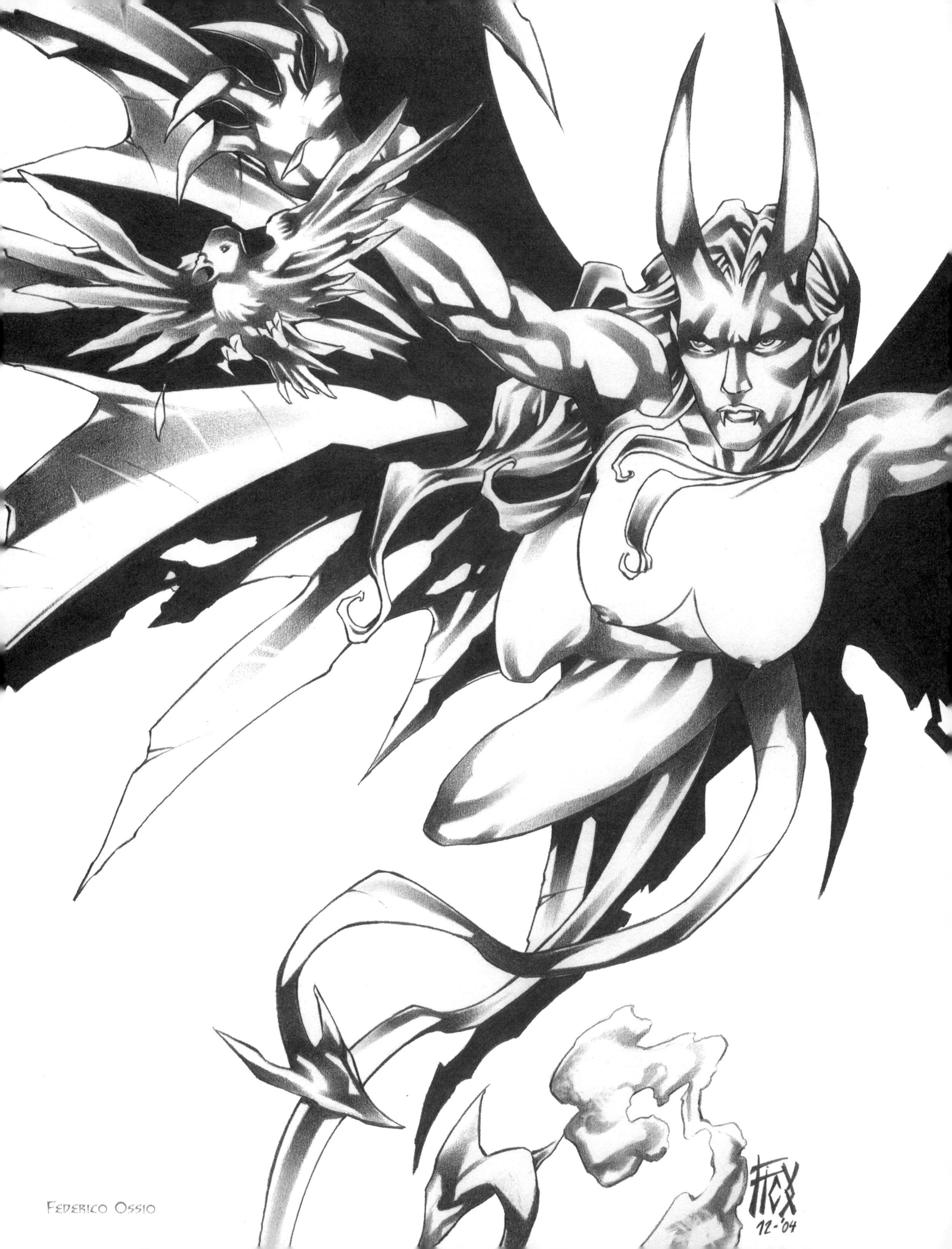

Federico Ossio

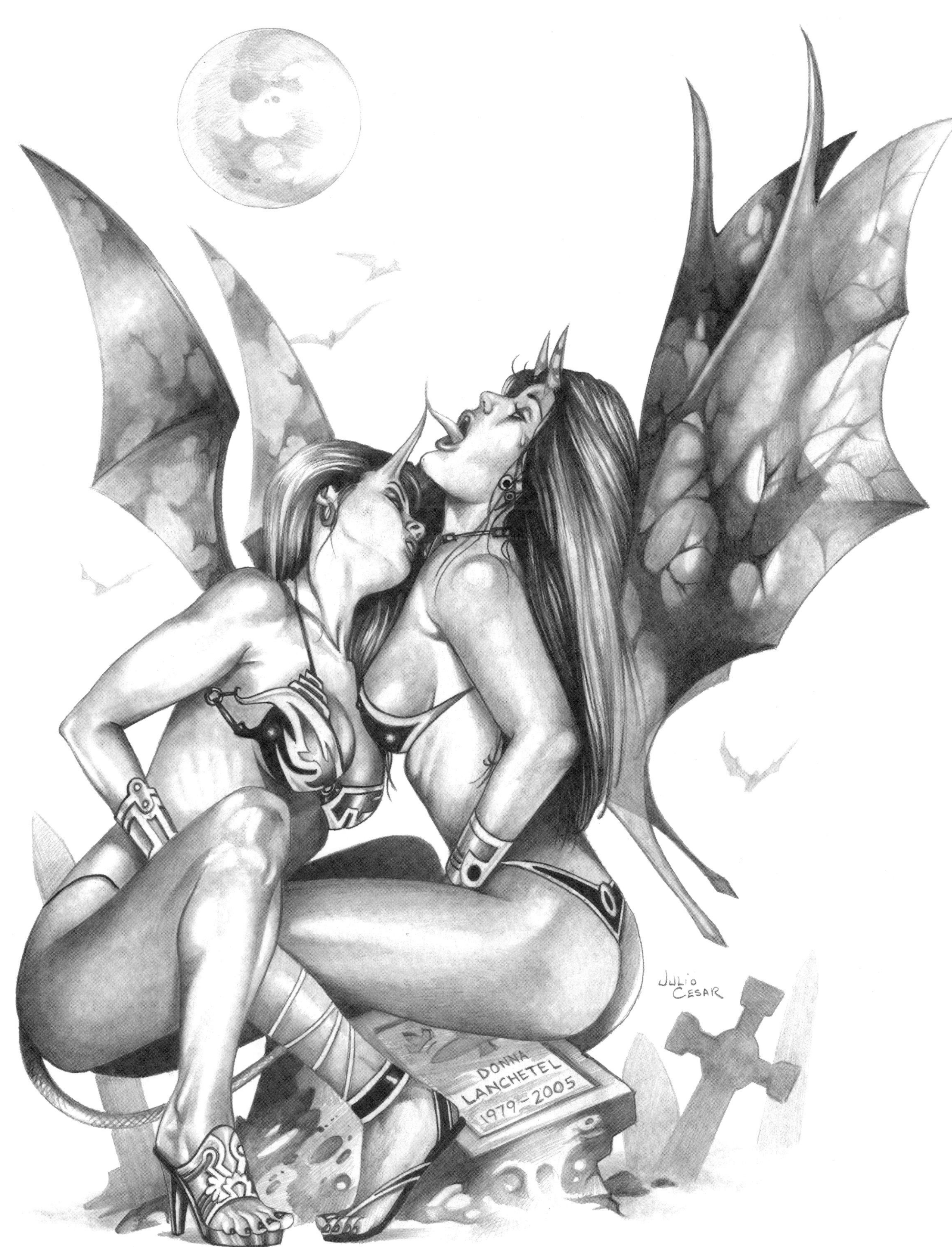

JULIO CESAR

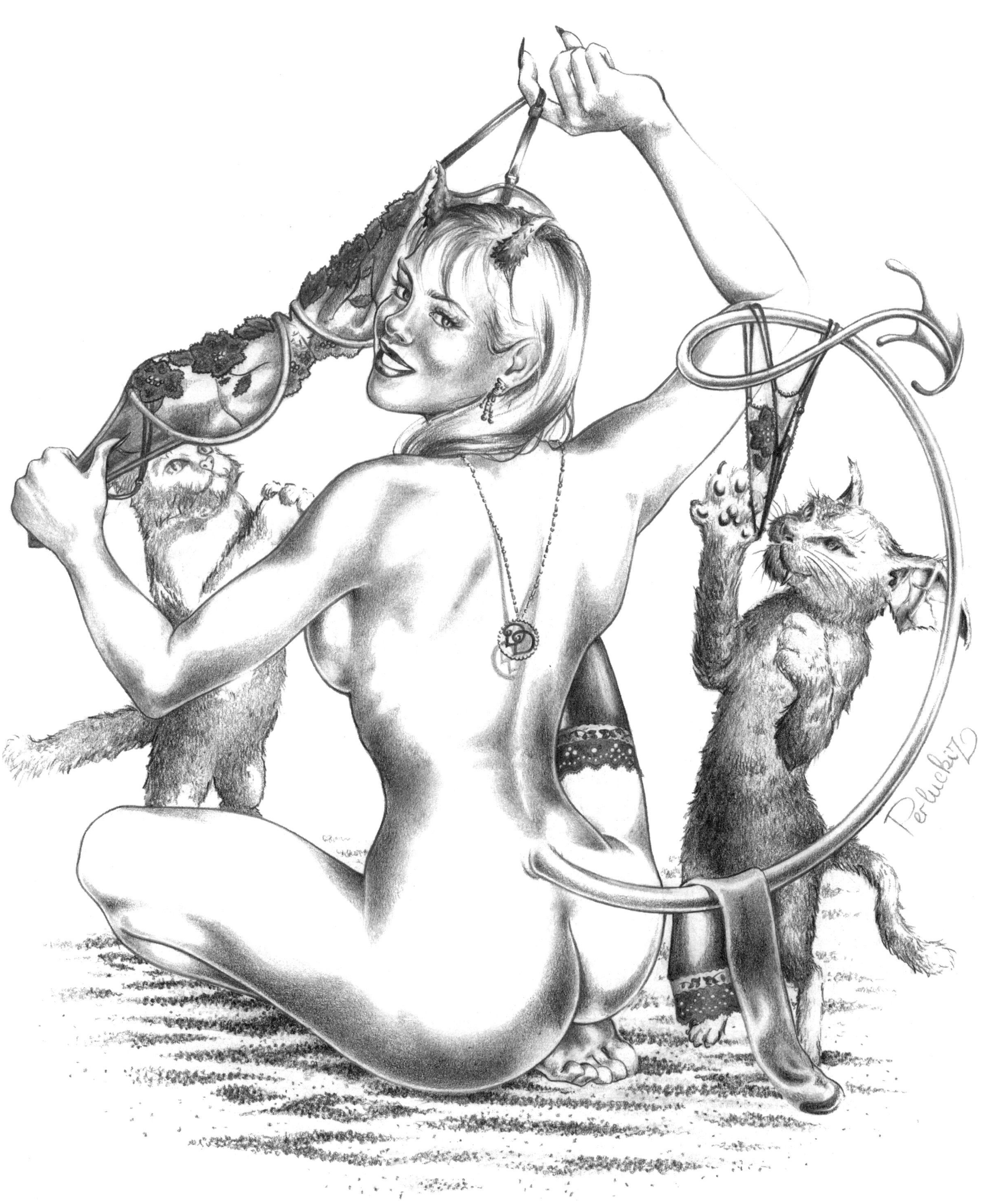

Perla Perlucky

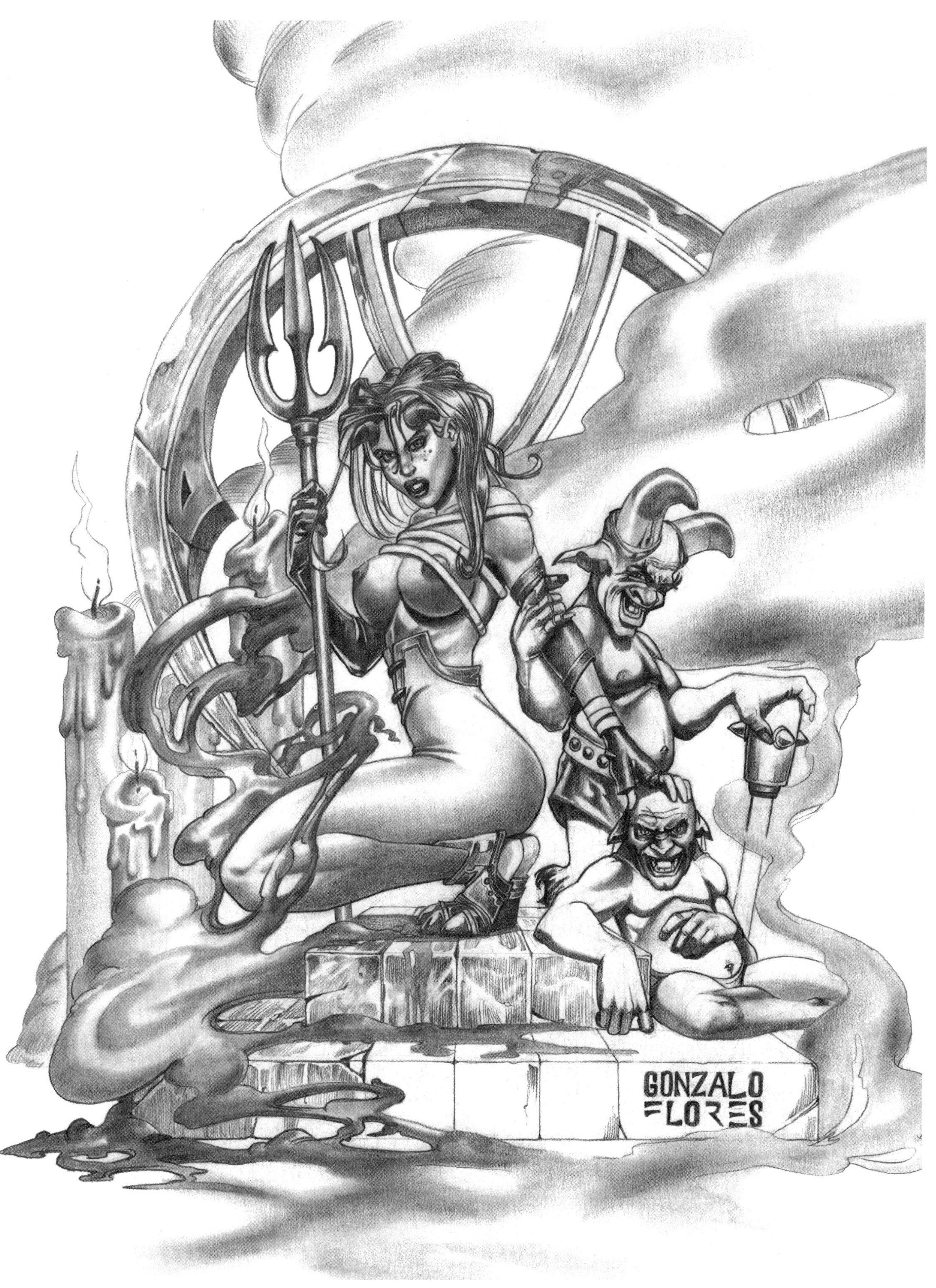

GONZALO FLORES

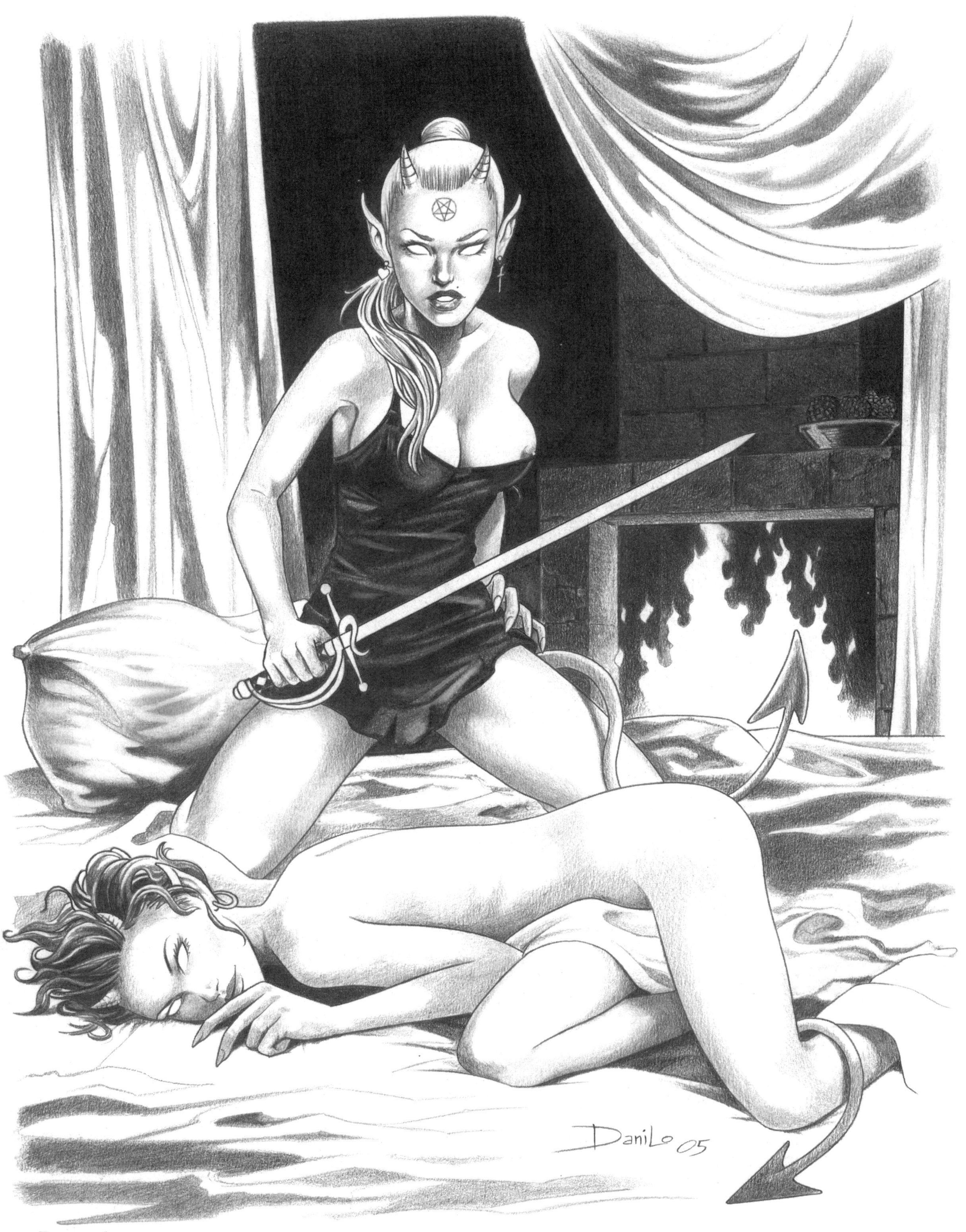

DANILO GUIDA

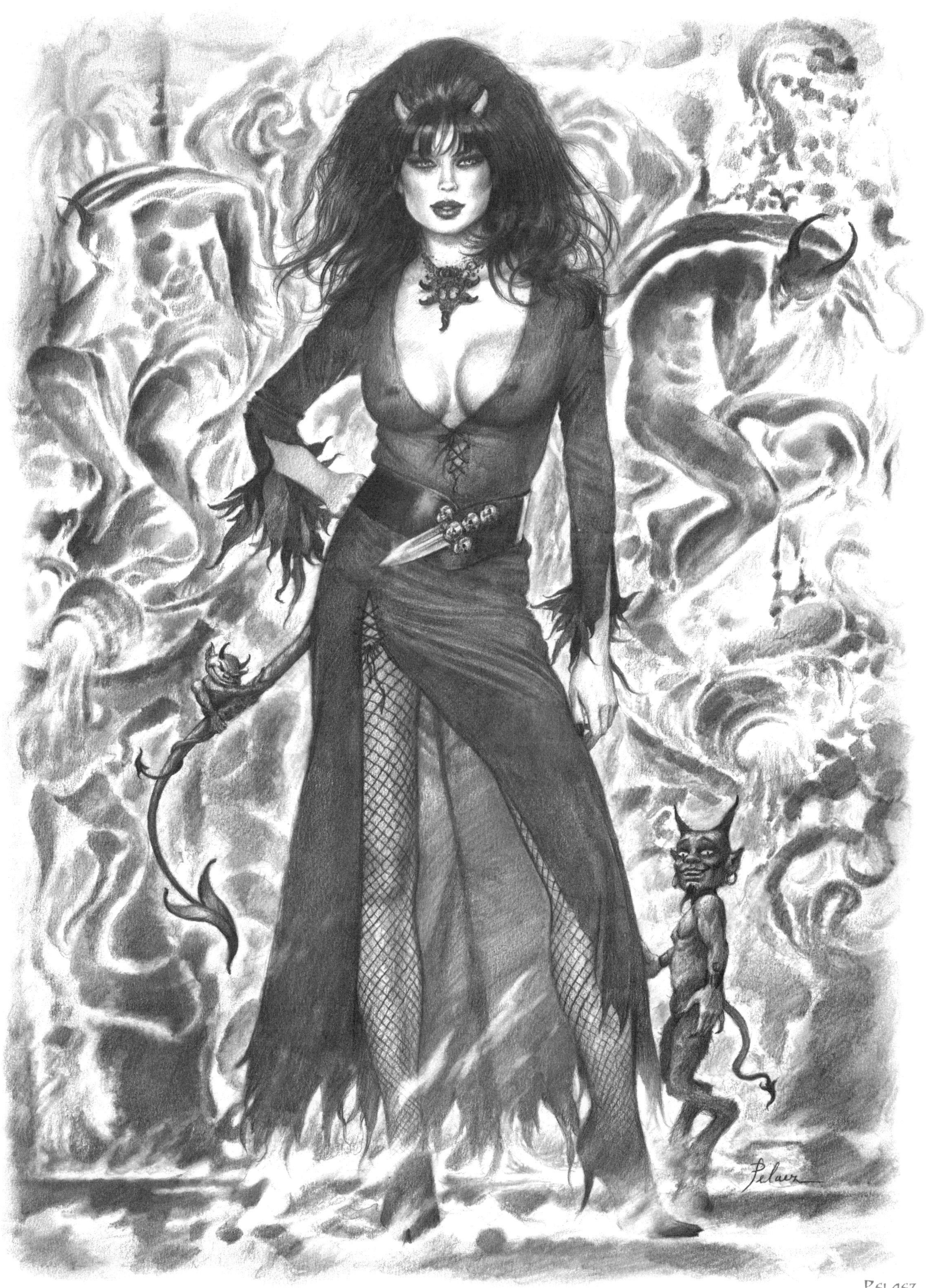

PELAEZ

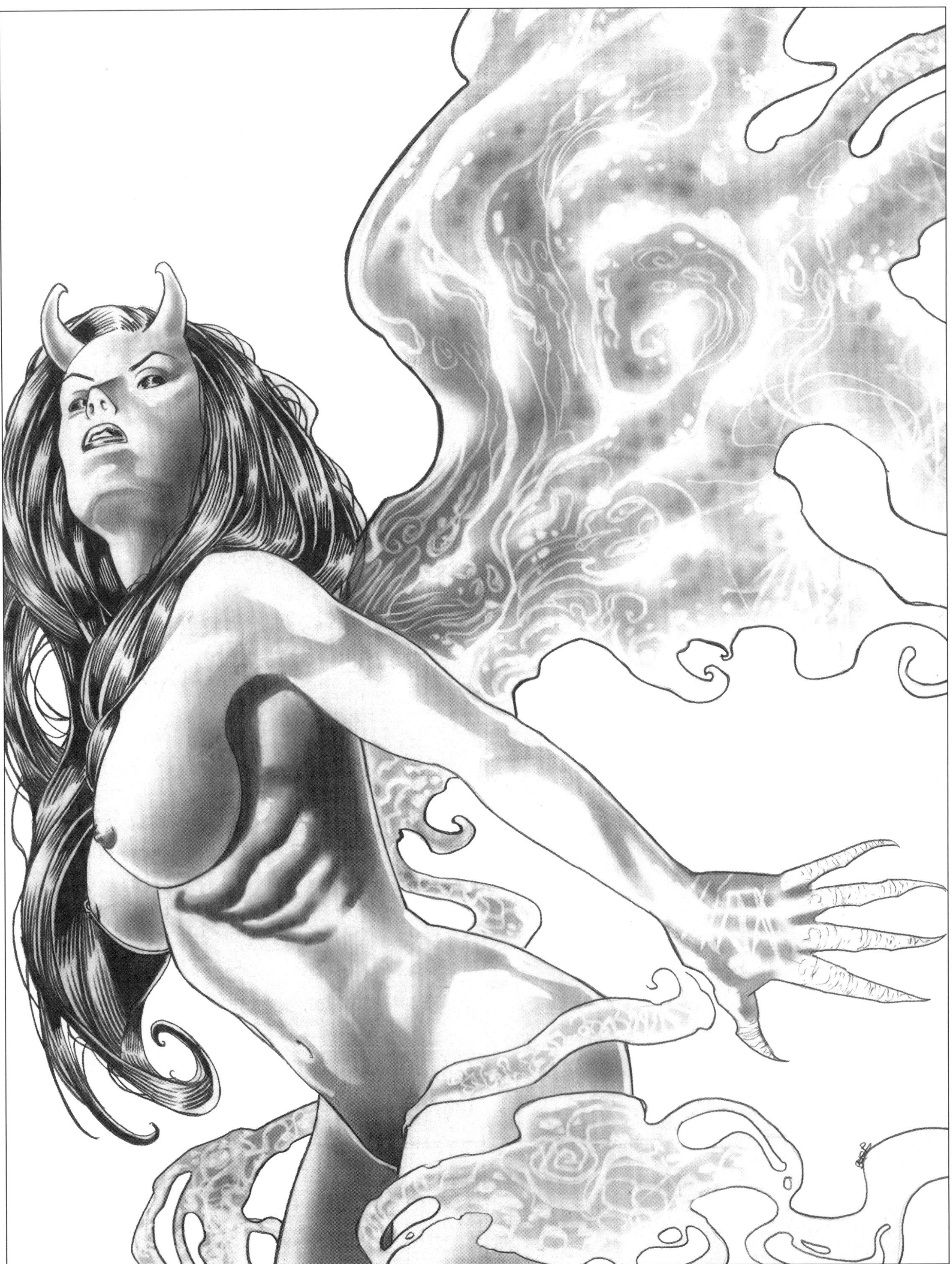

Buci

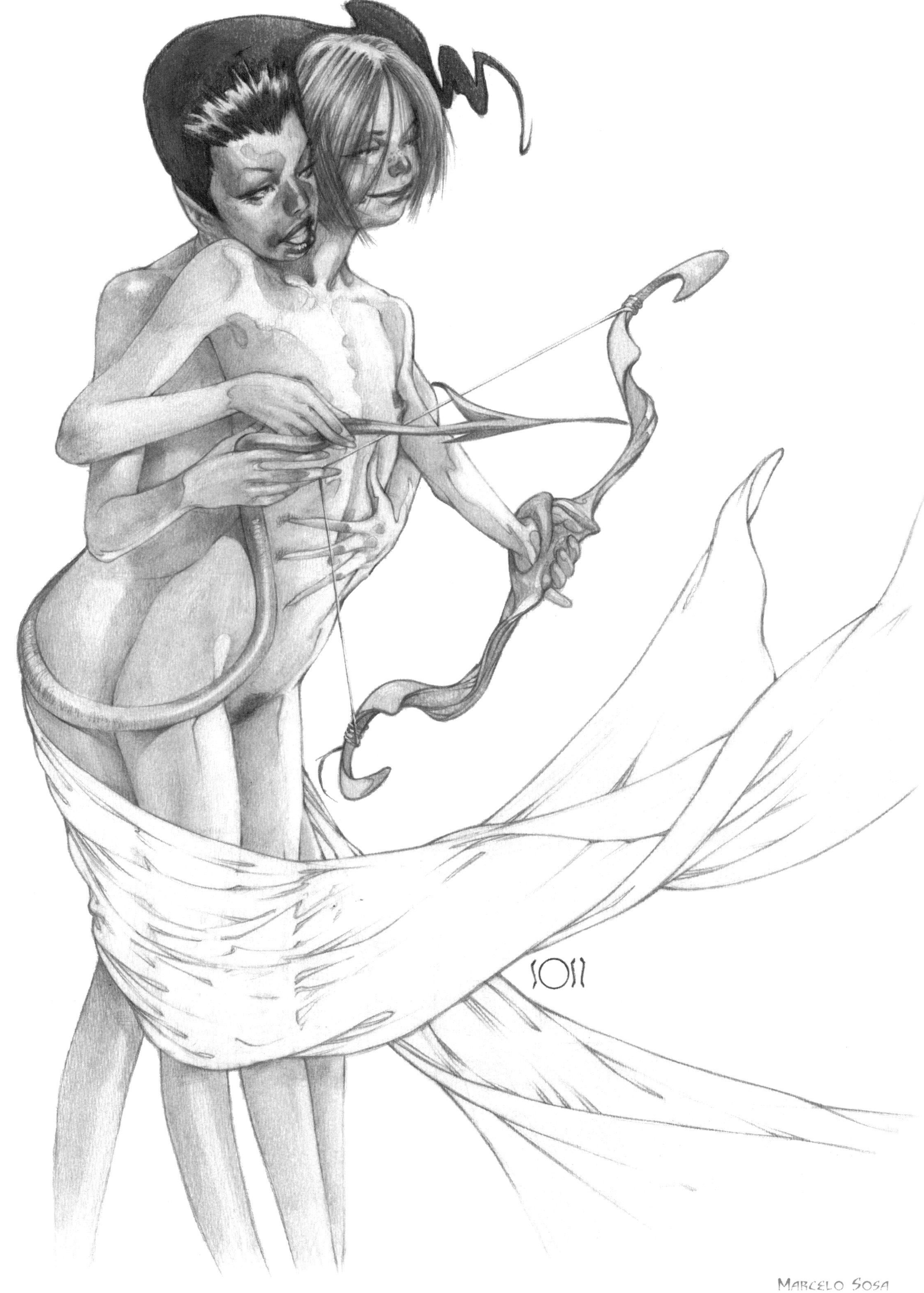

Marcelo Sosa

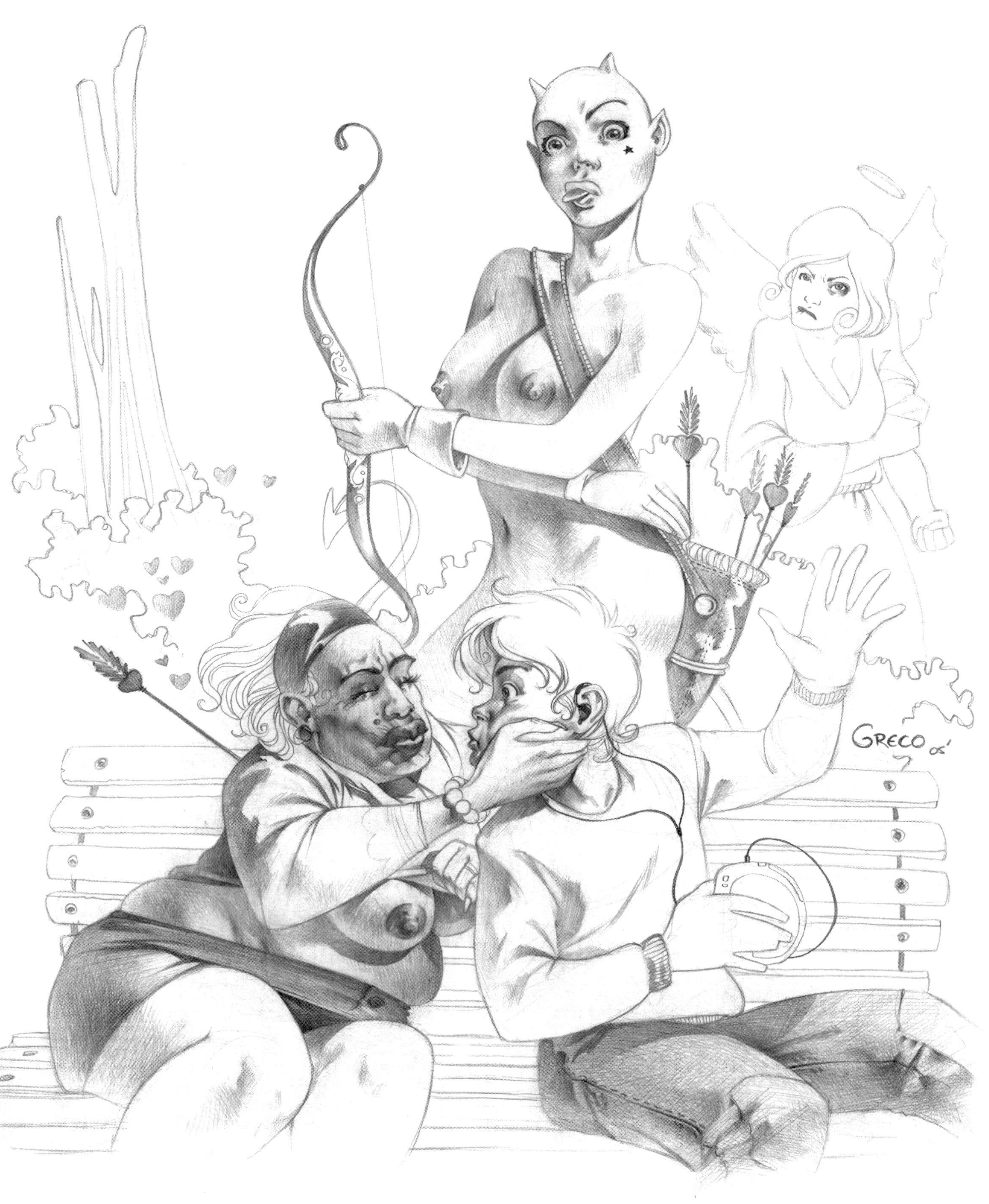

DIEGO GRECO

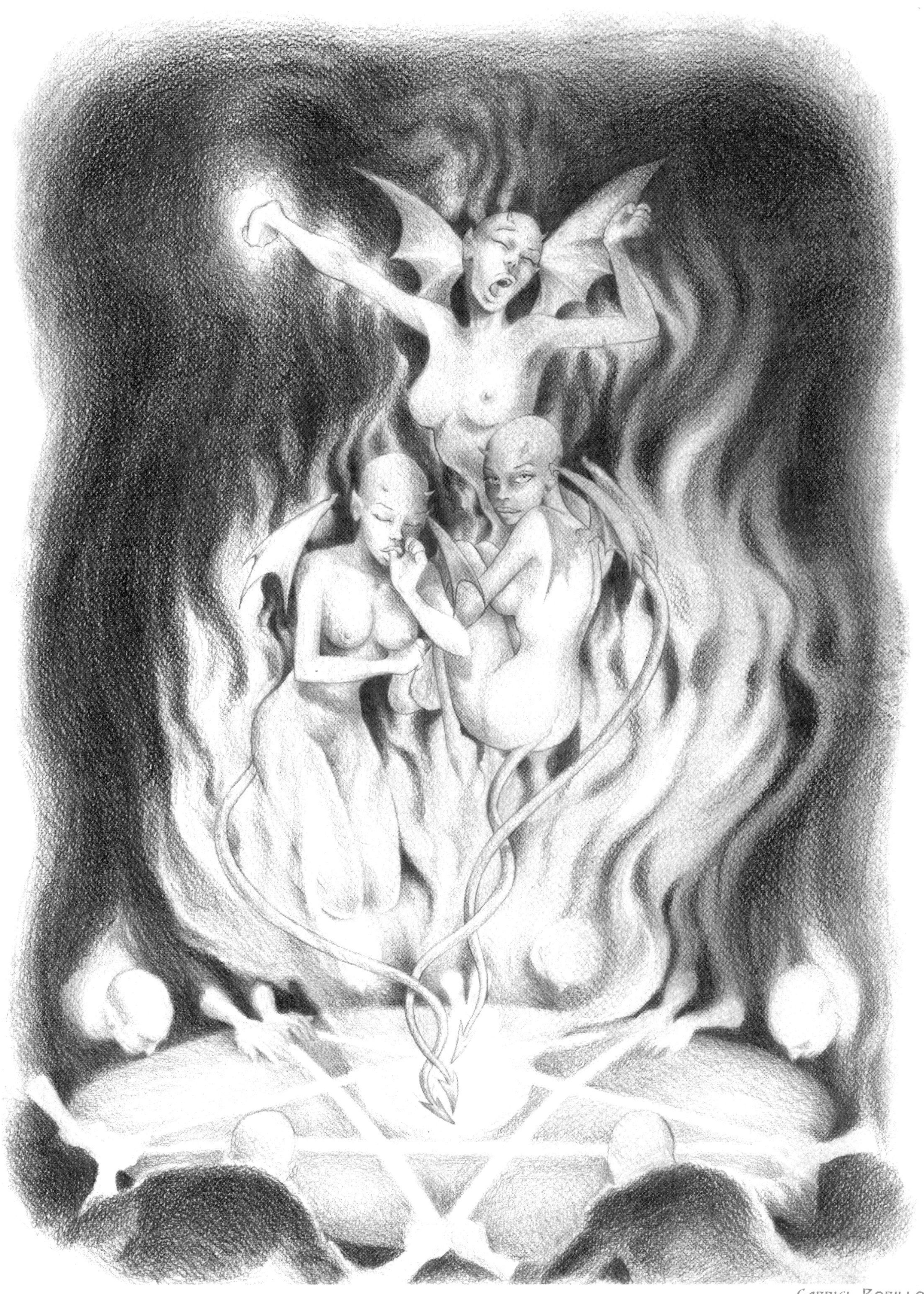

Gabriel Bobillo

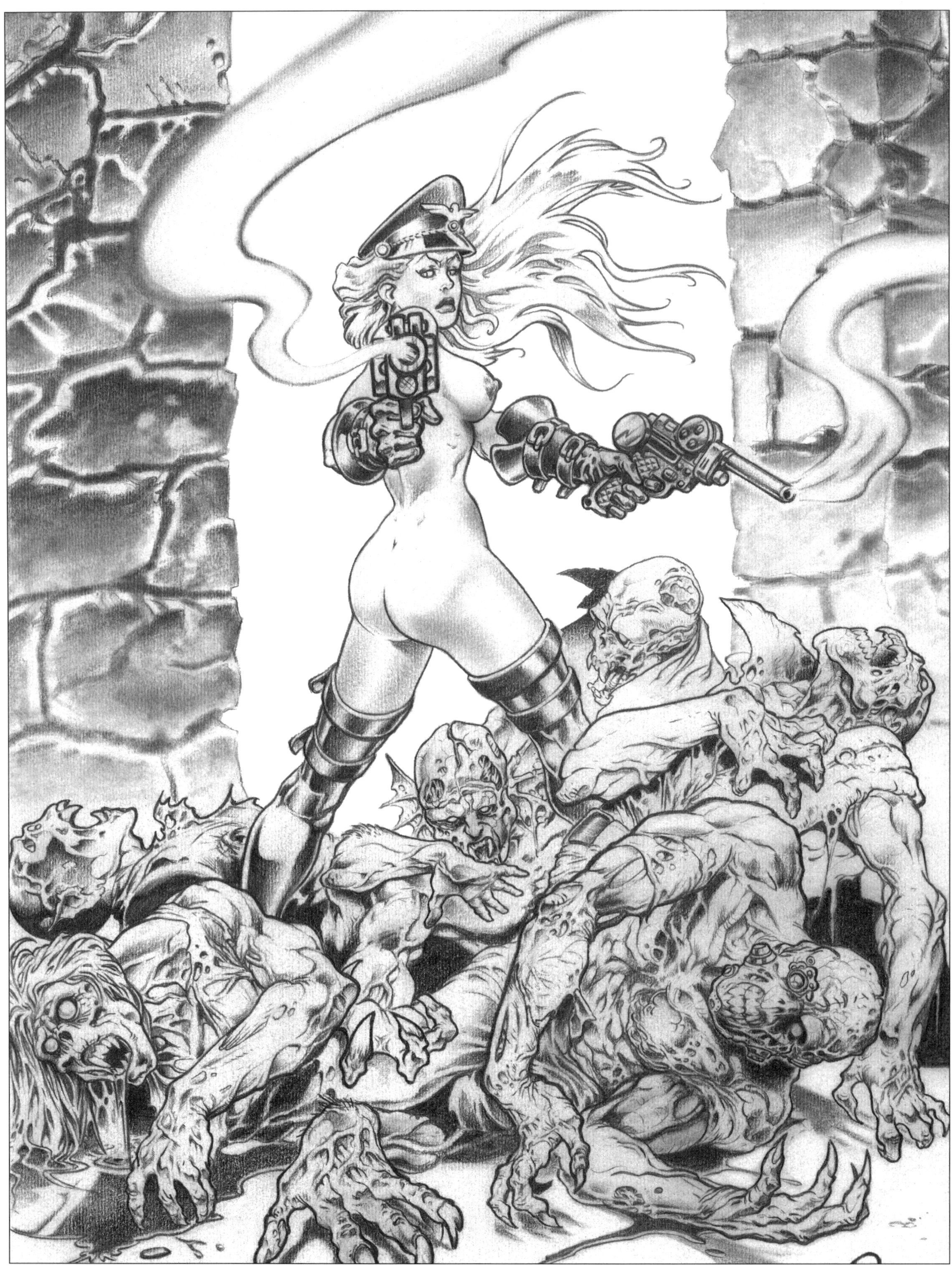

German Ponce

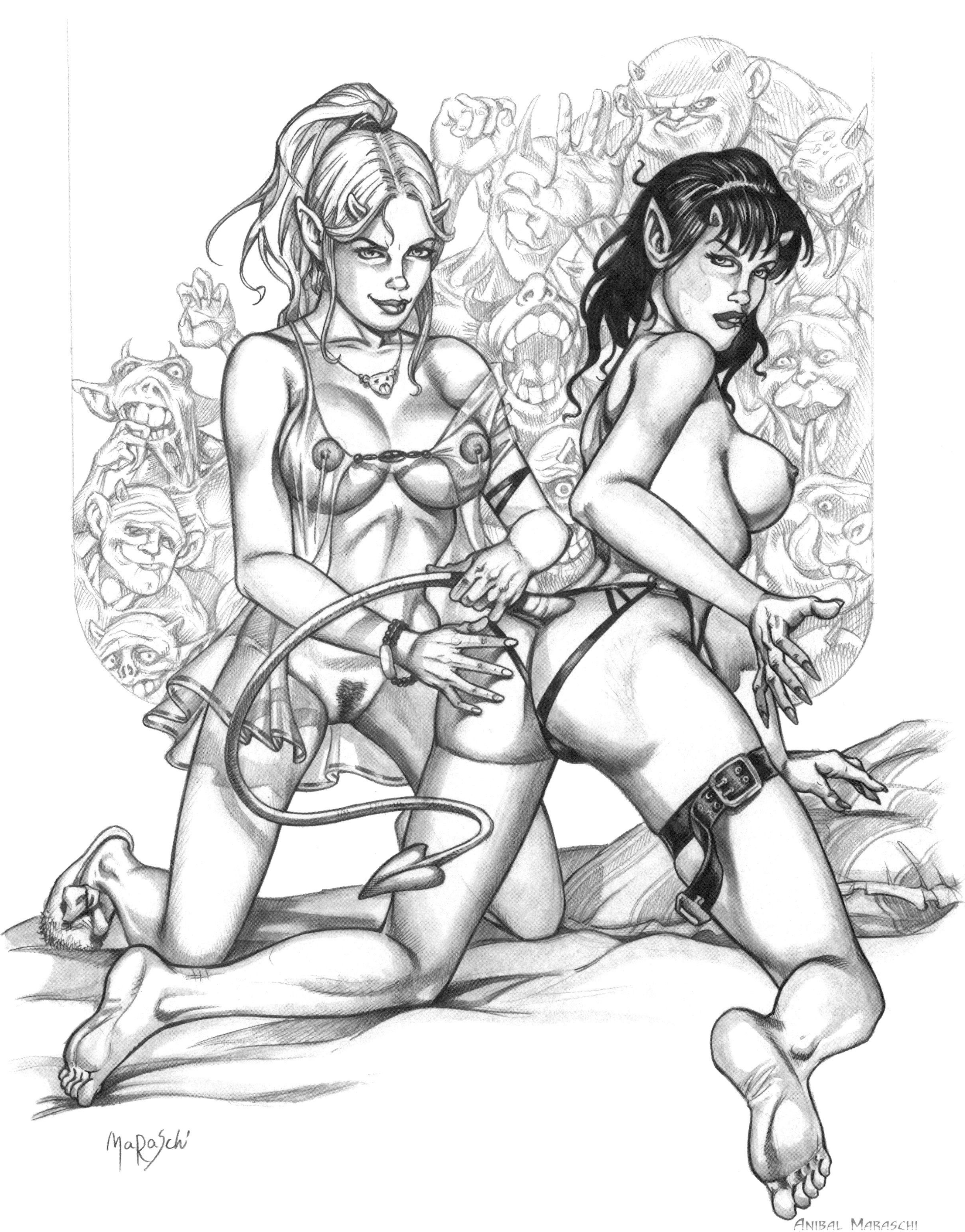

ANIBAL MARASCHI

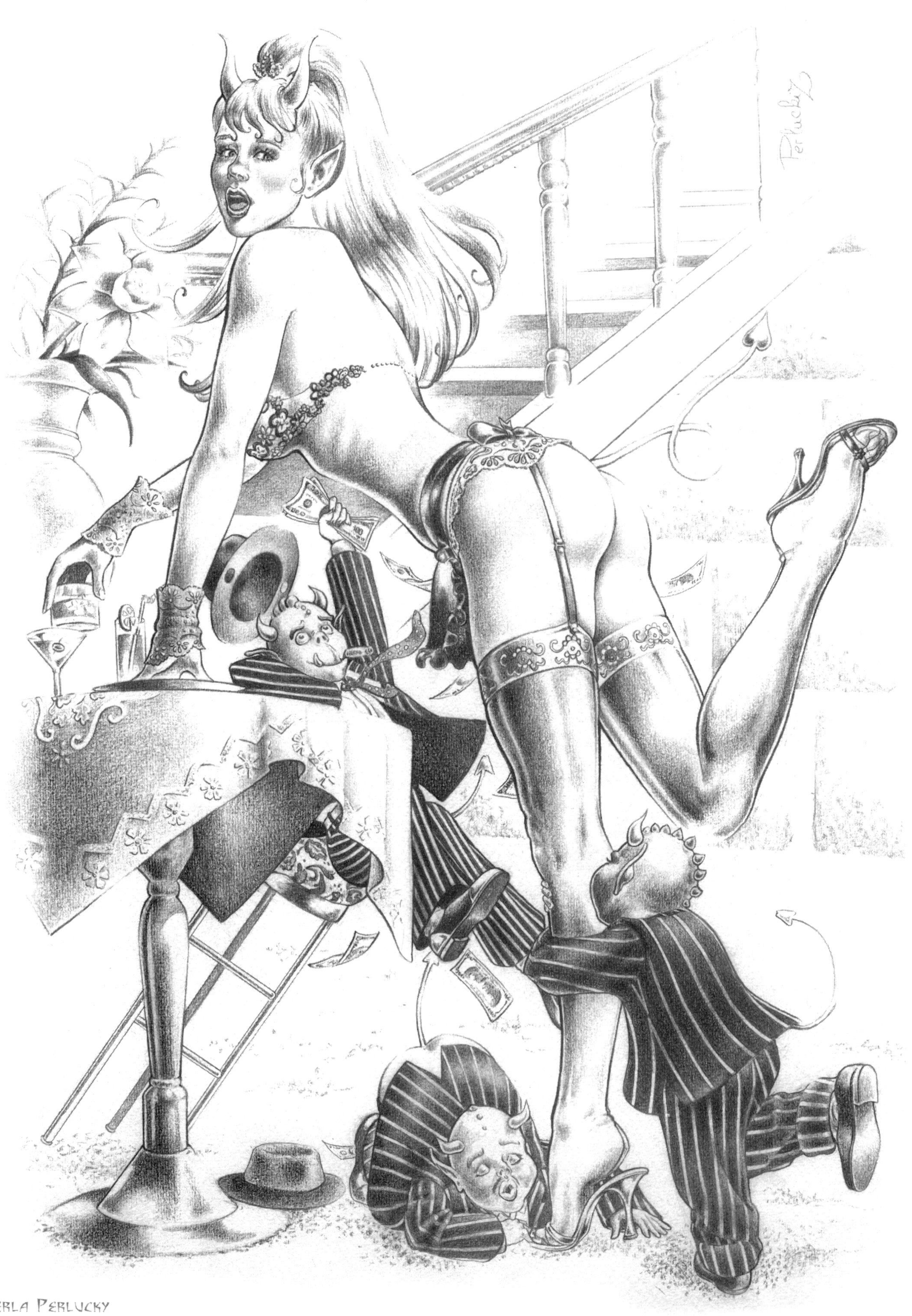

Perla Perlucky

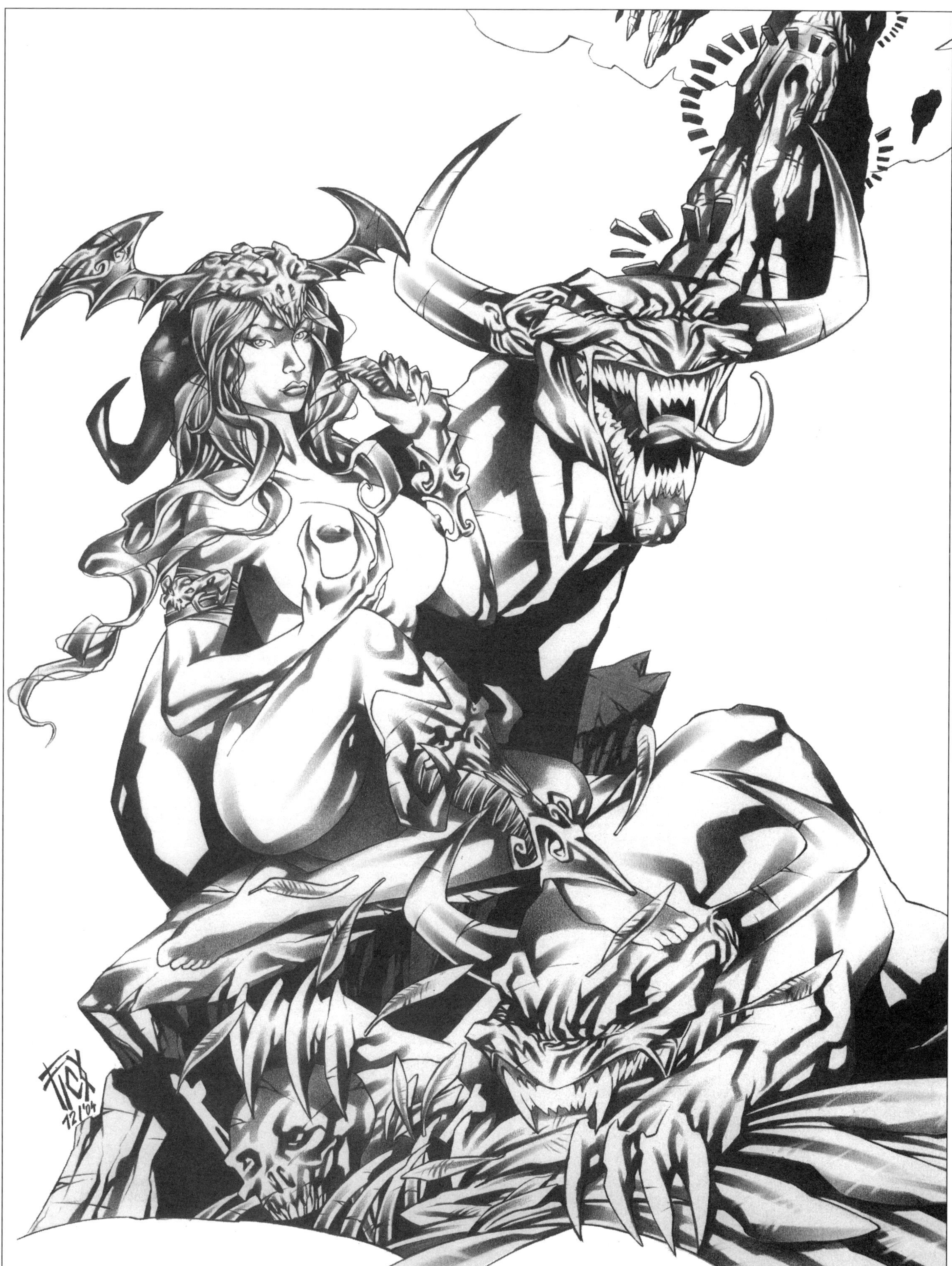

Federico Ossio

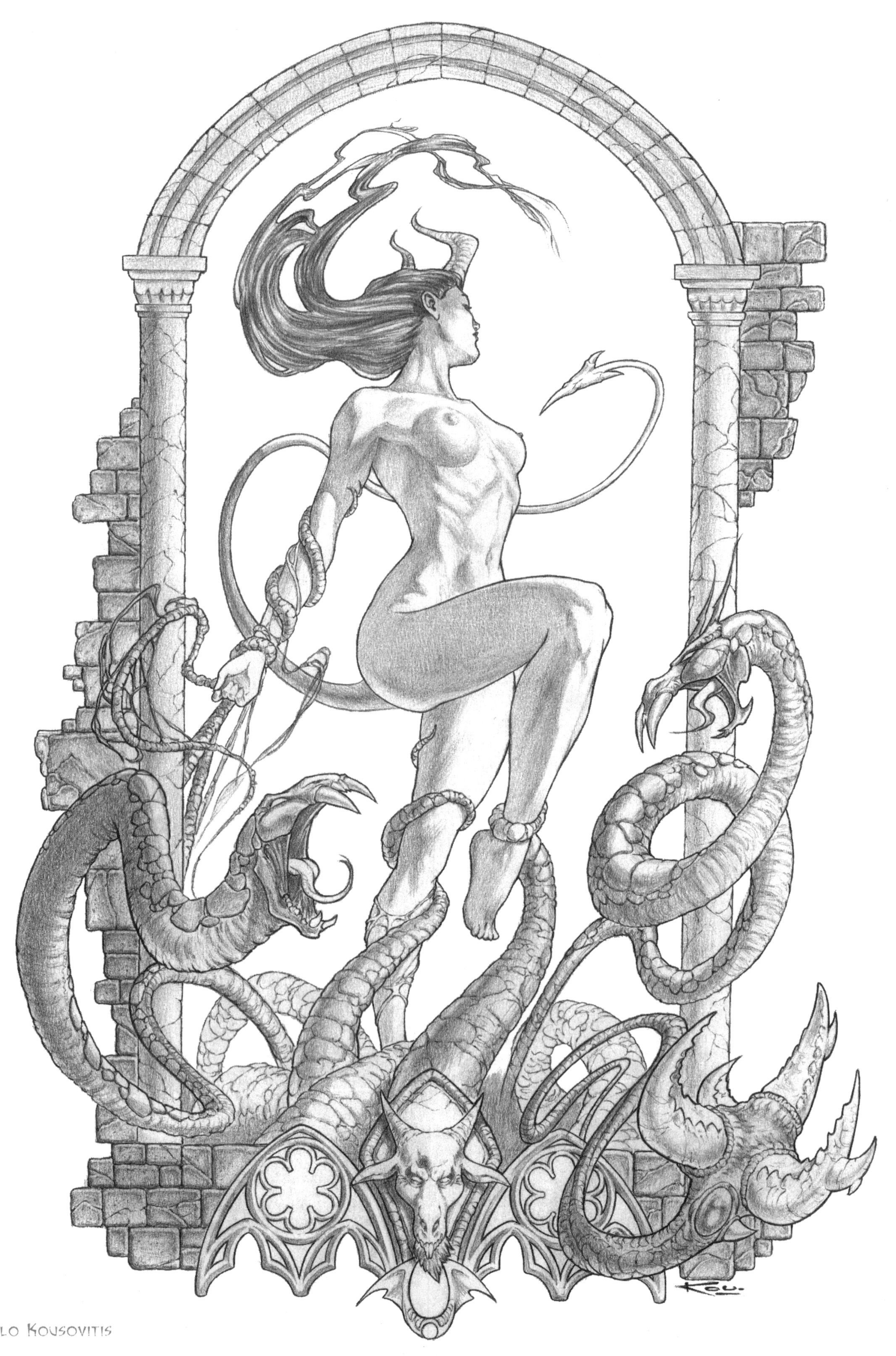

Pablo Kousovitis

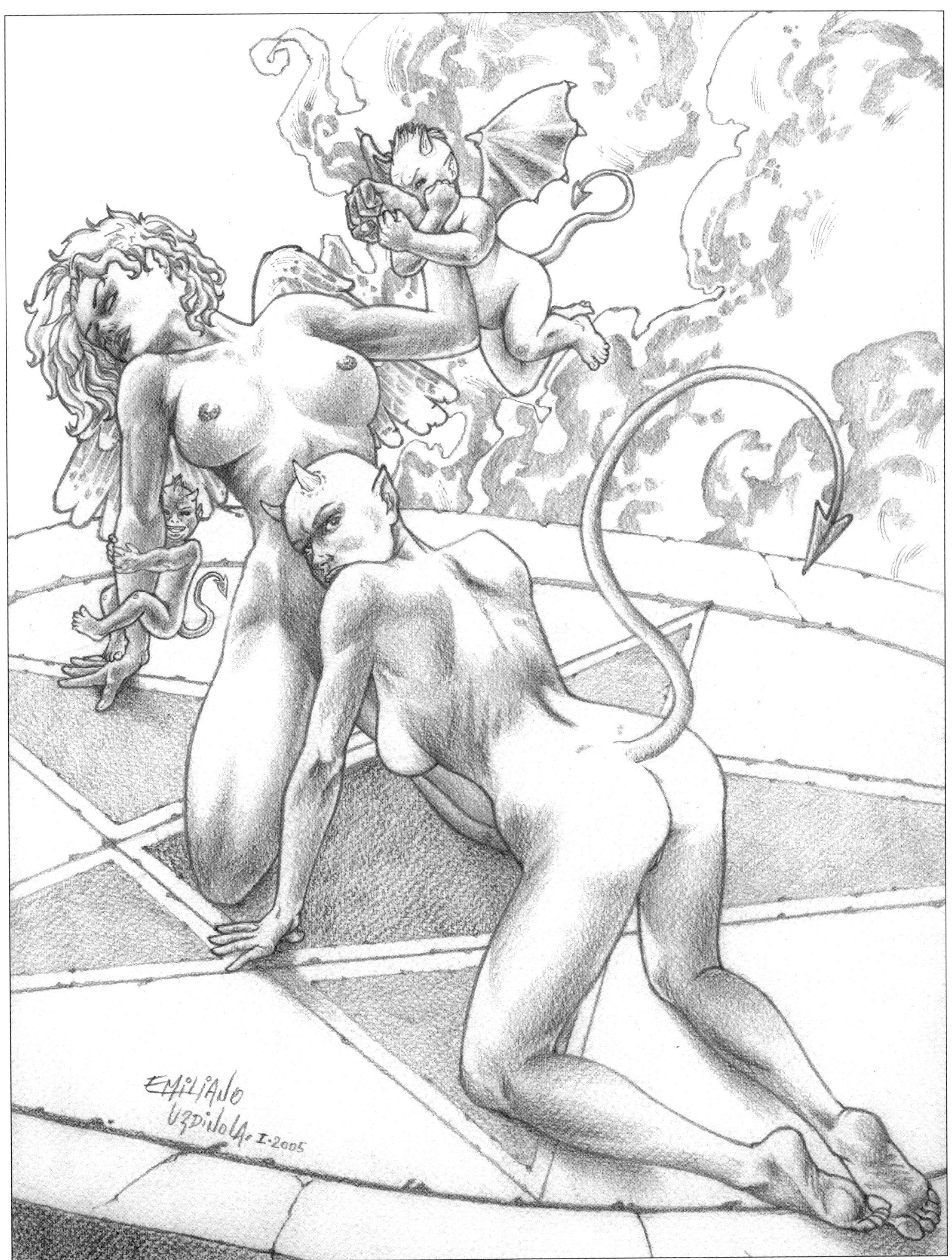

Emiliano Urdinola

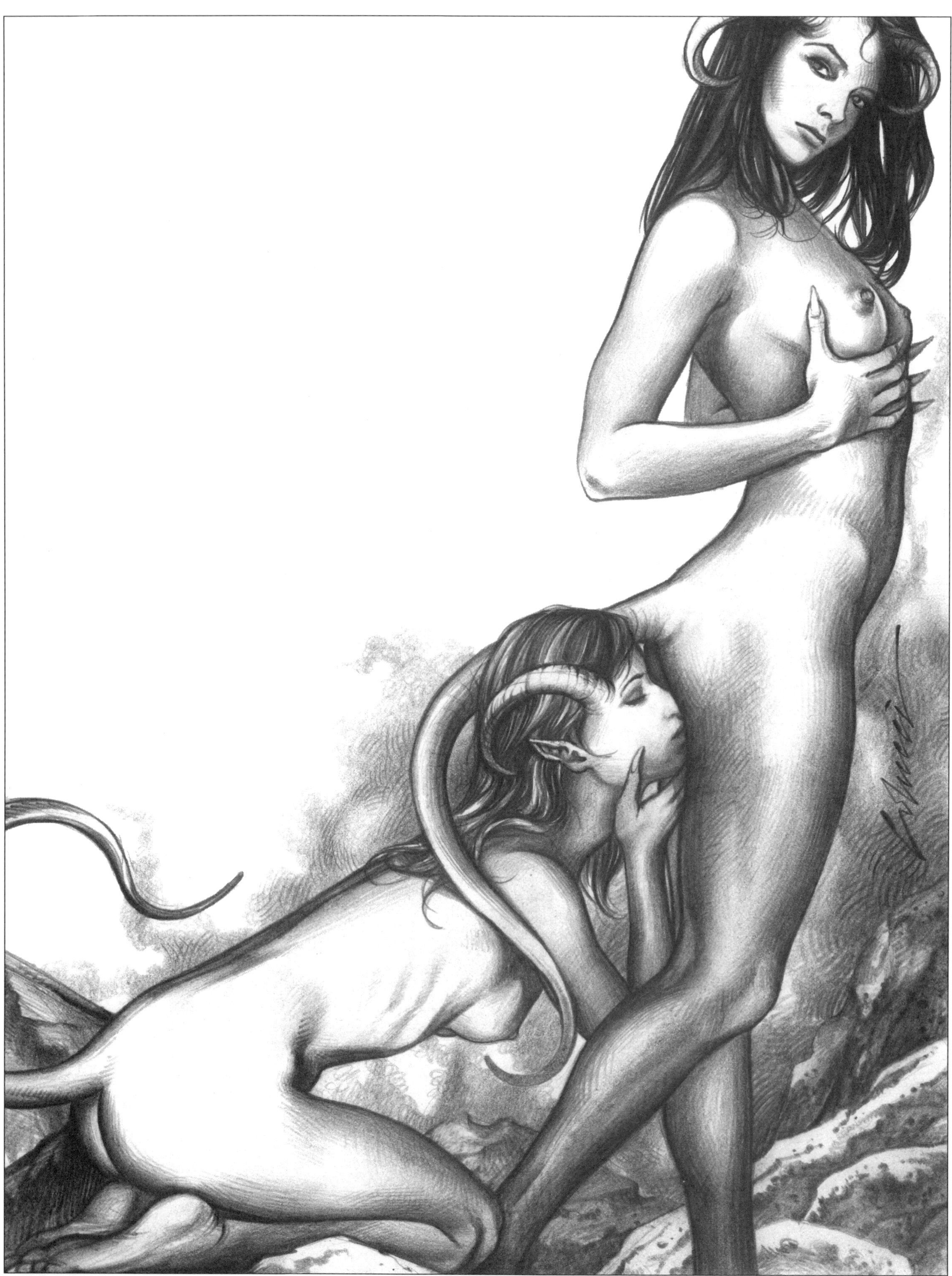

ALEJANDRO COLUCCI

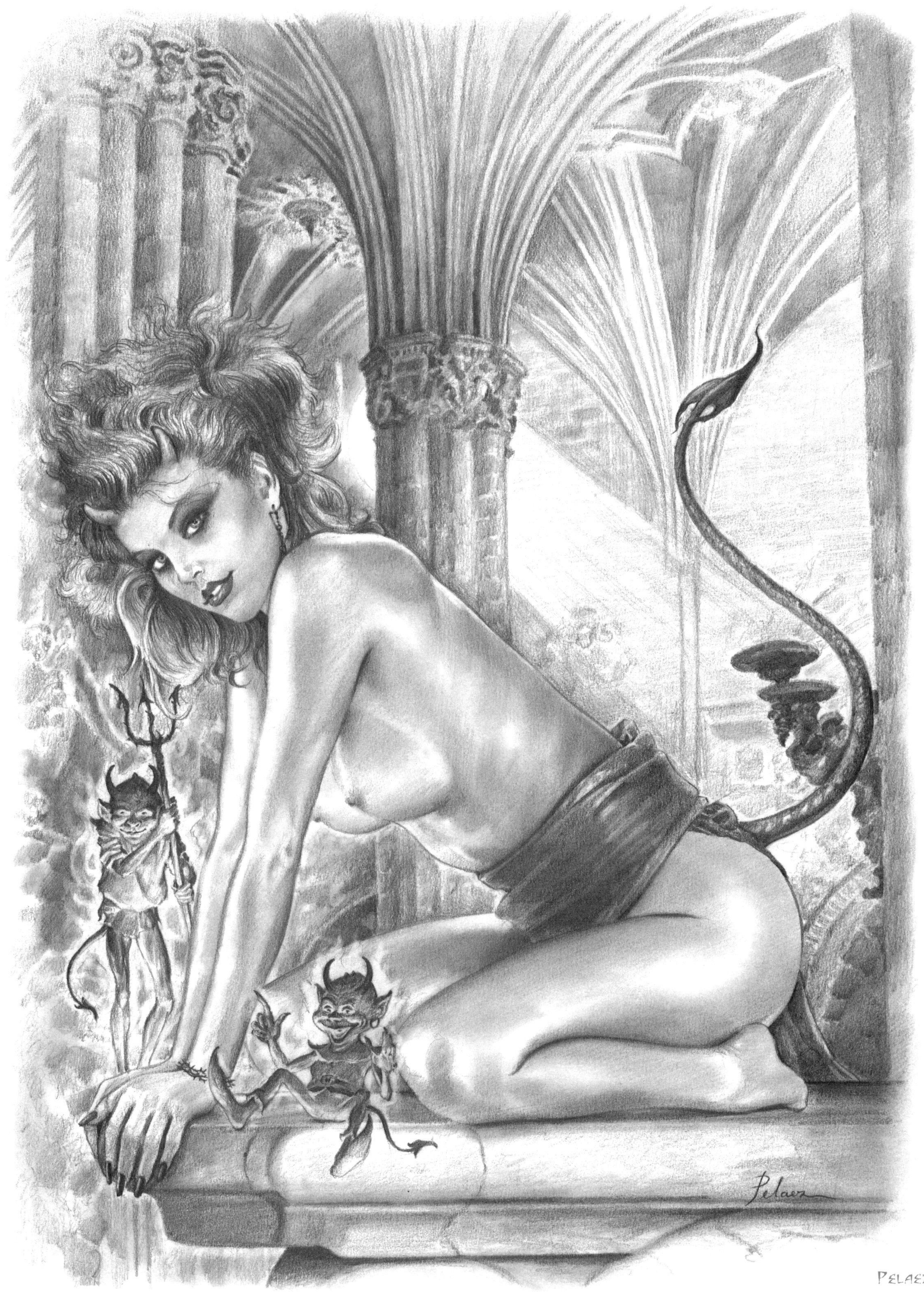

PELAEZ

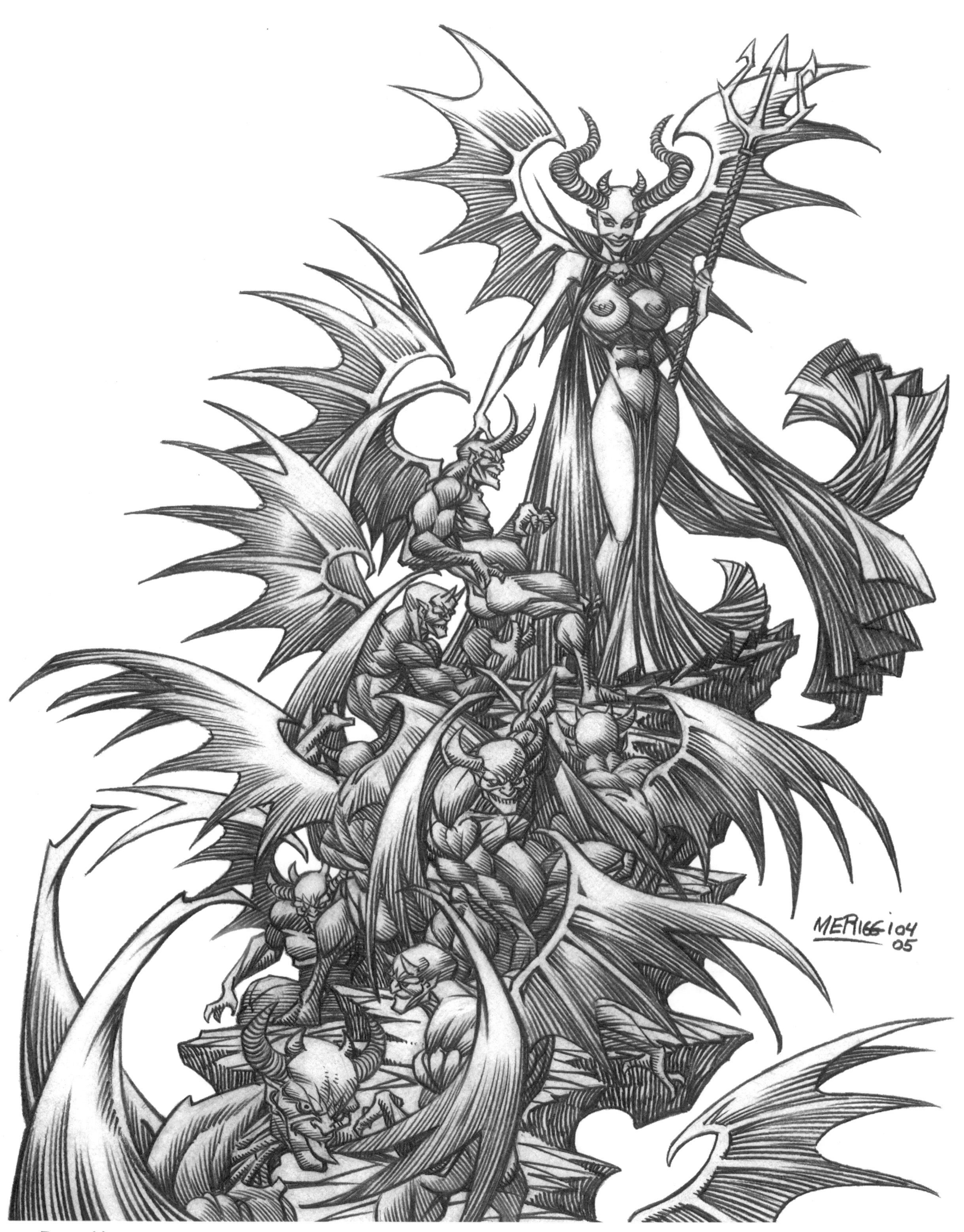

RUBEN MERIGGI

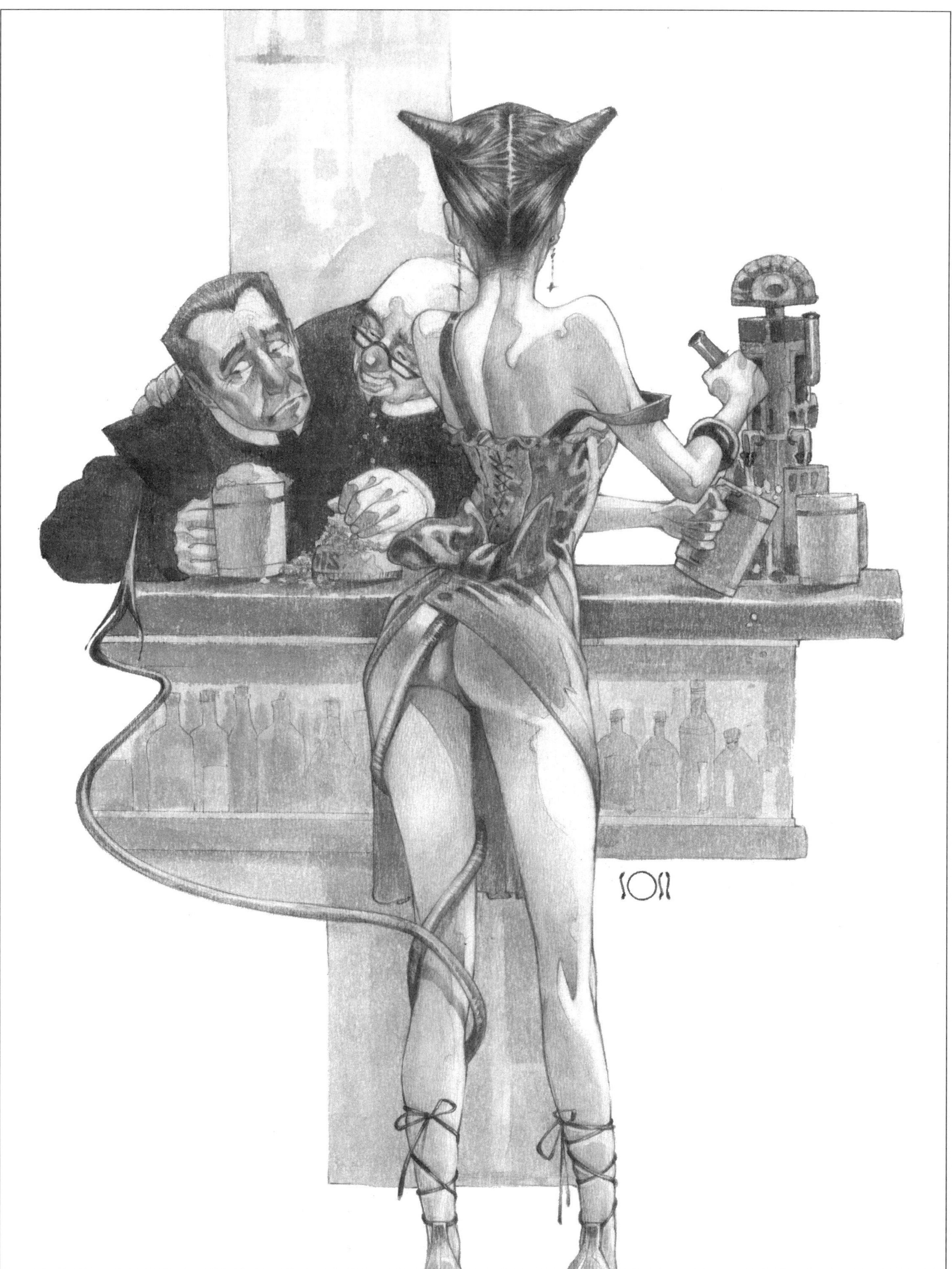

Marcelo Sosa

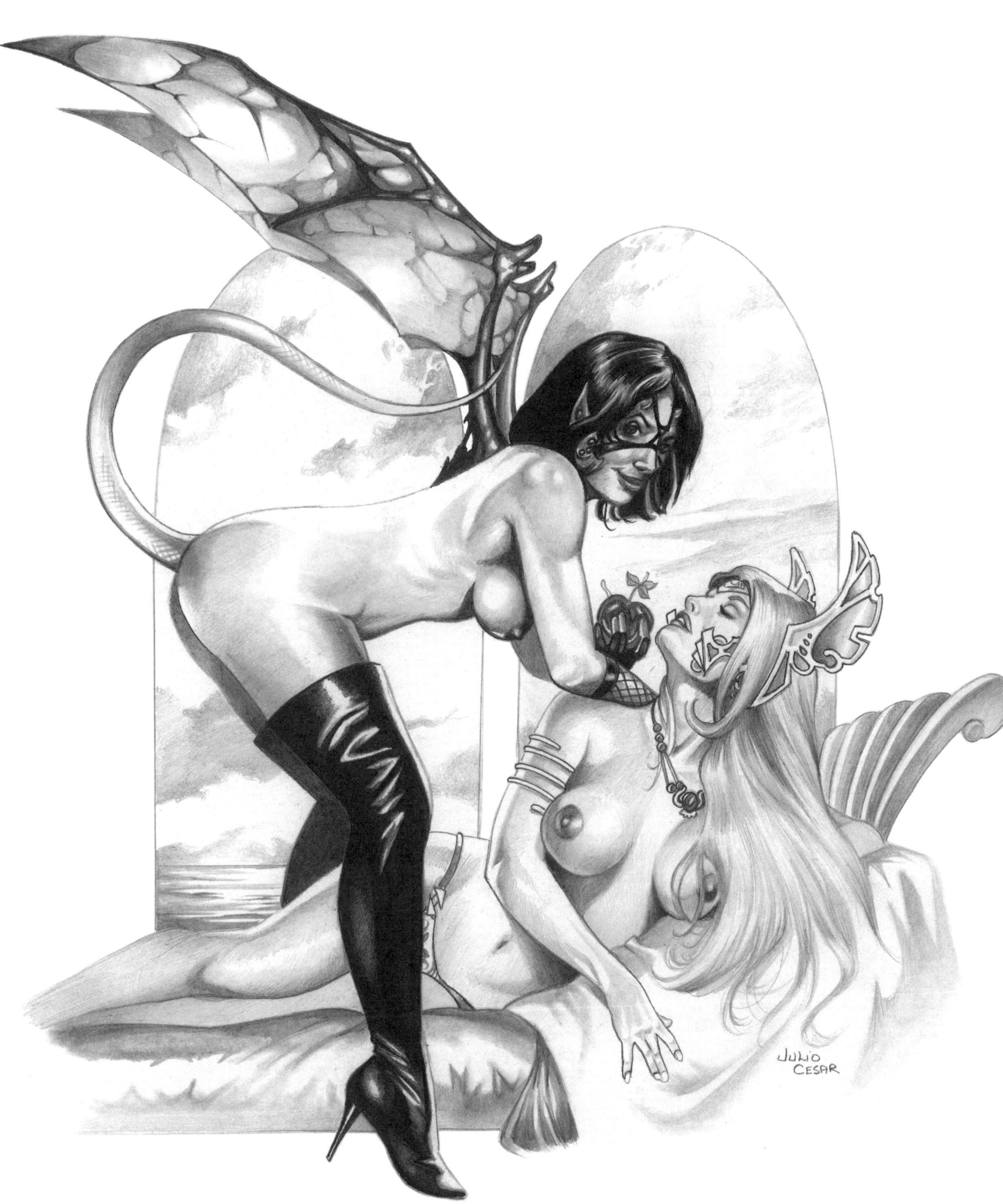

JULIO CESAR

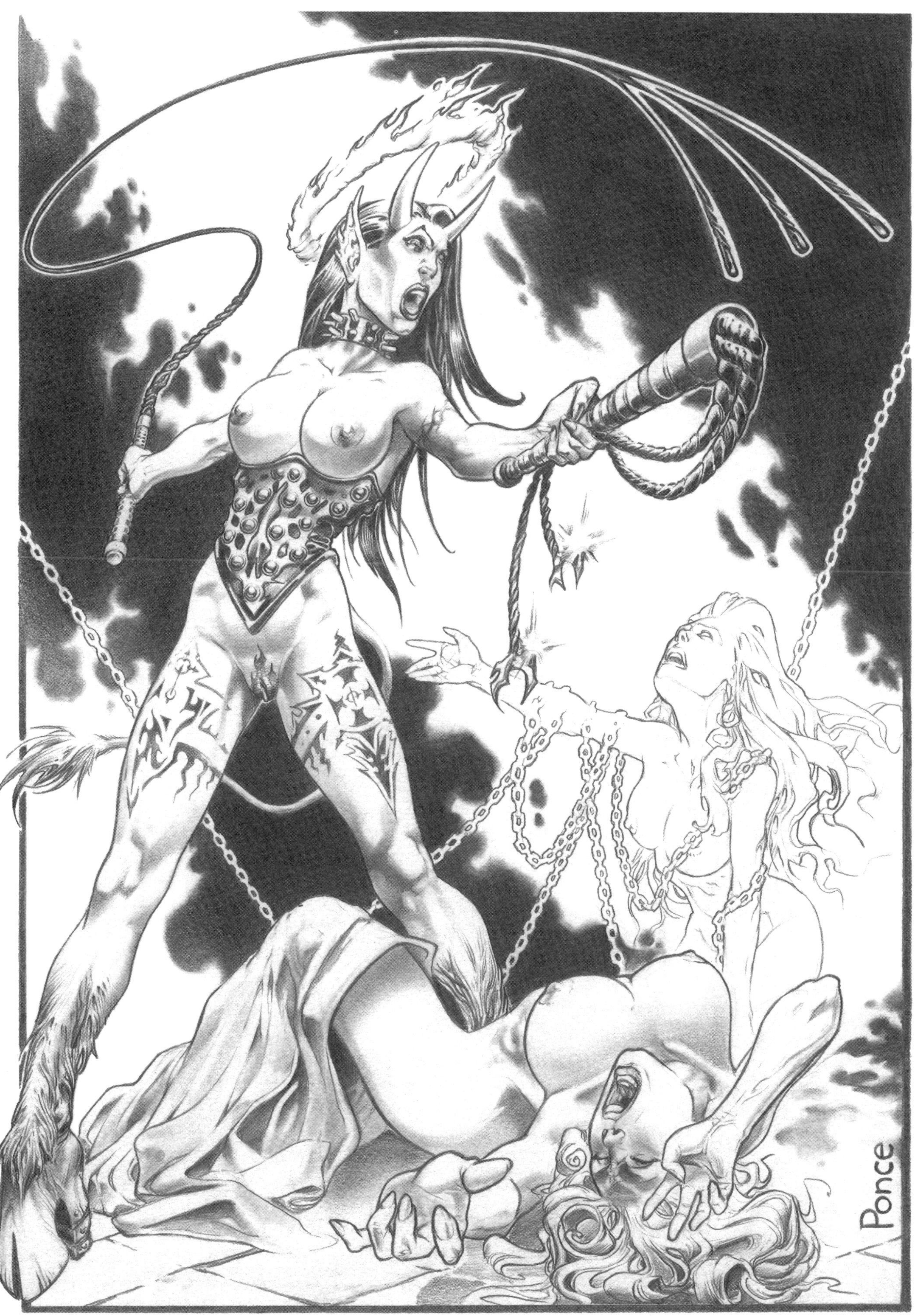

German Ponce

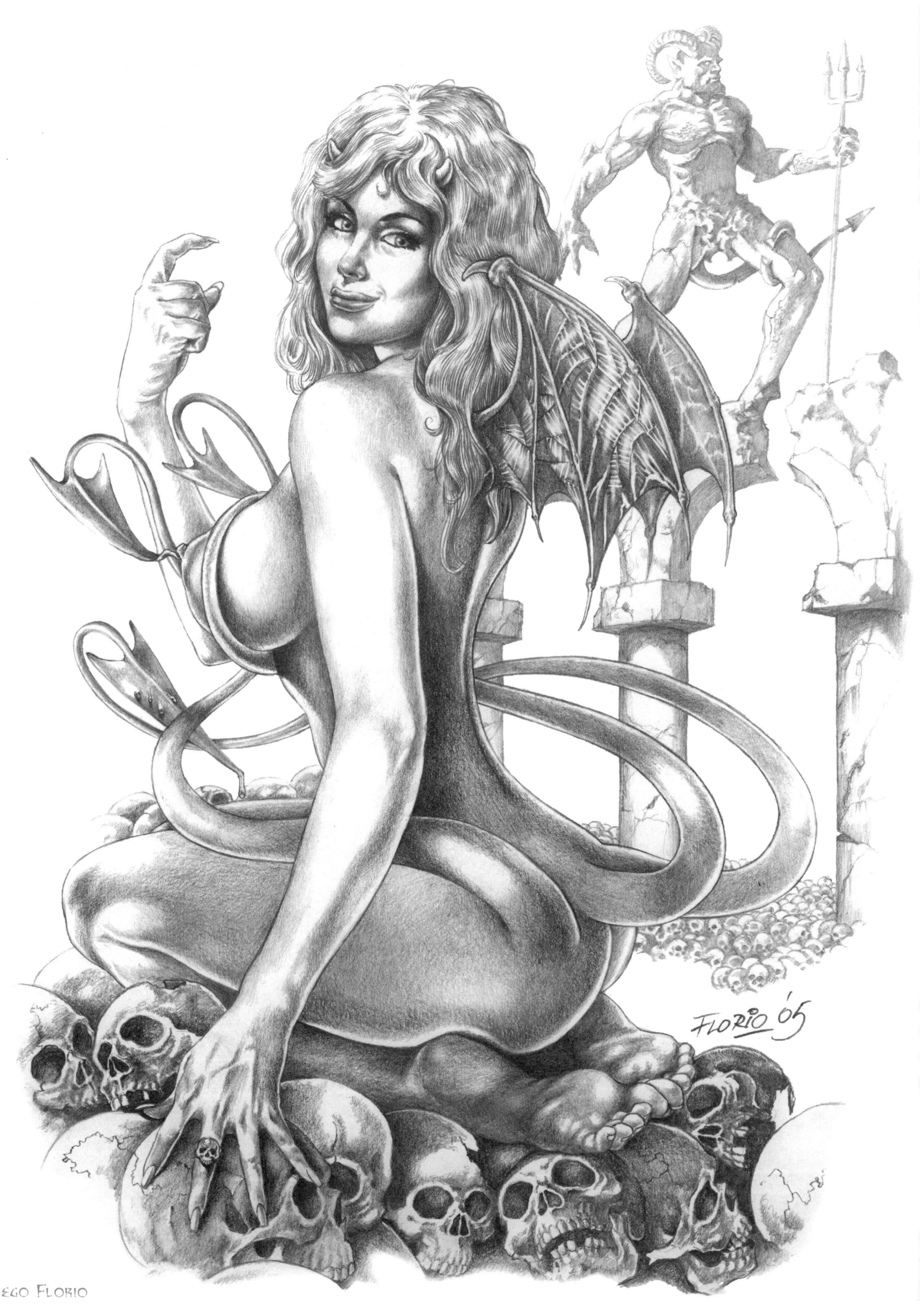

Diego Florio

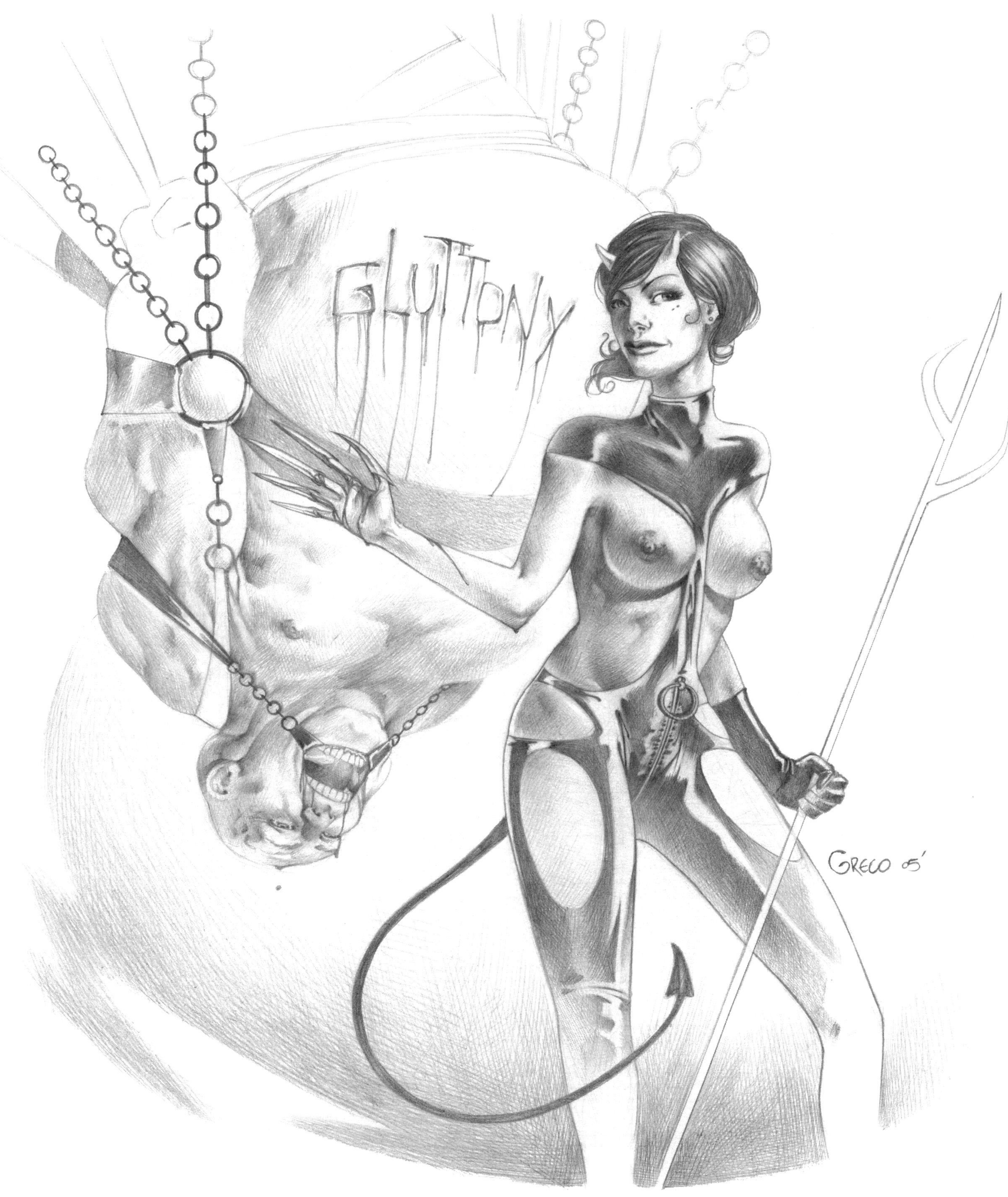

DIEGO GRECO

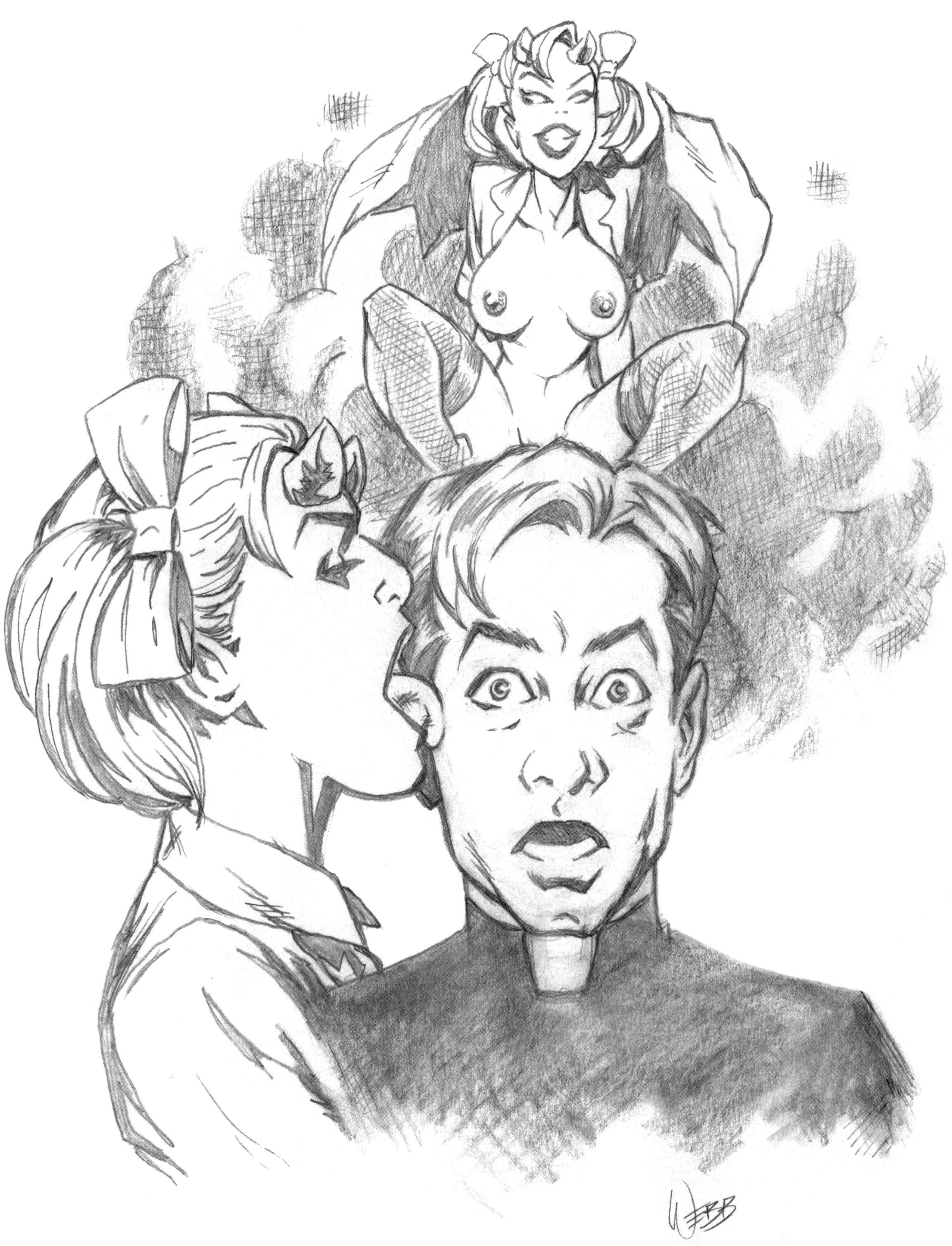

Jim Webb

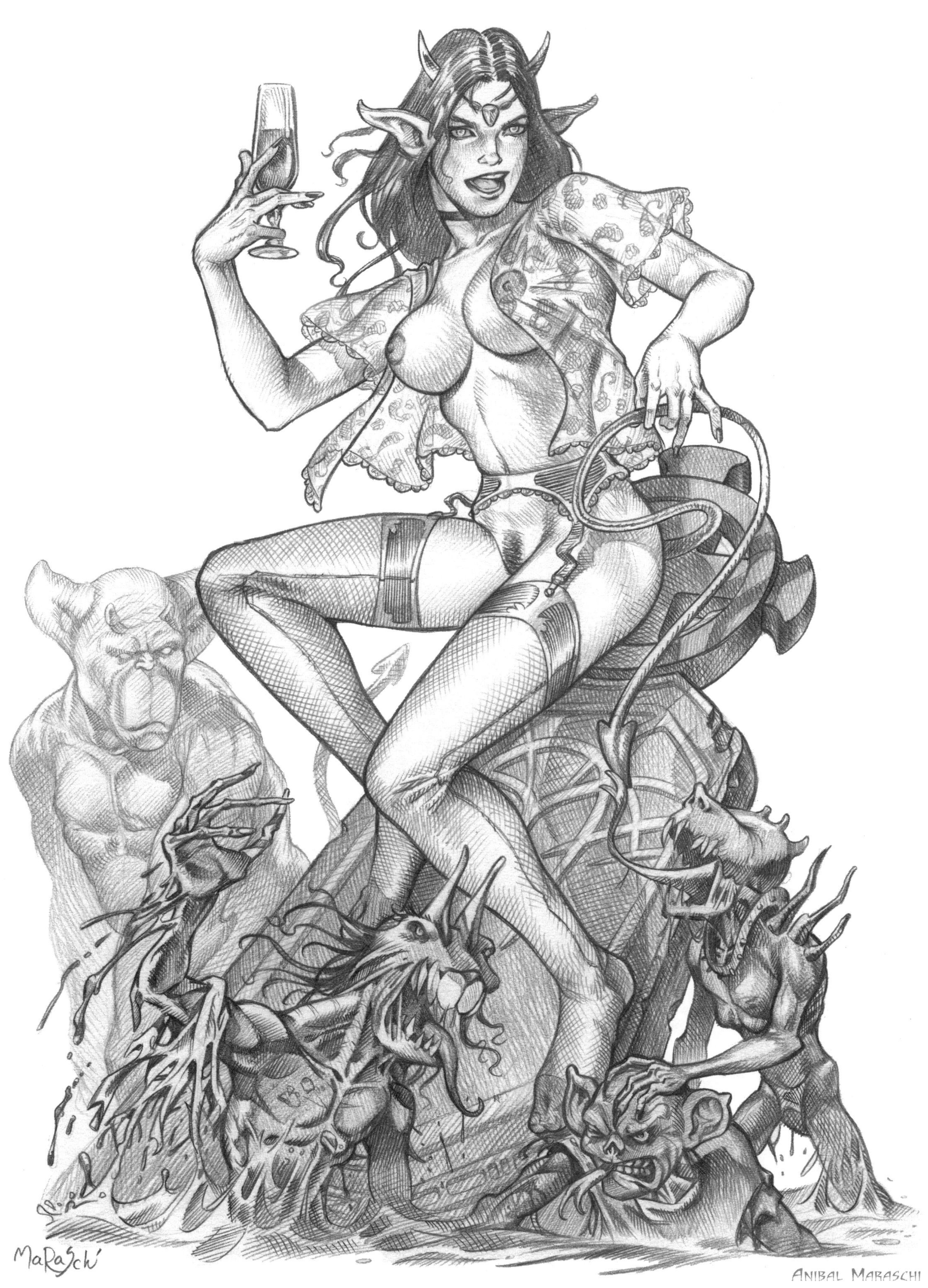
MaRaSchi
ANIBAL MARASCHI

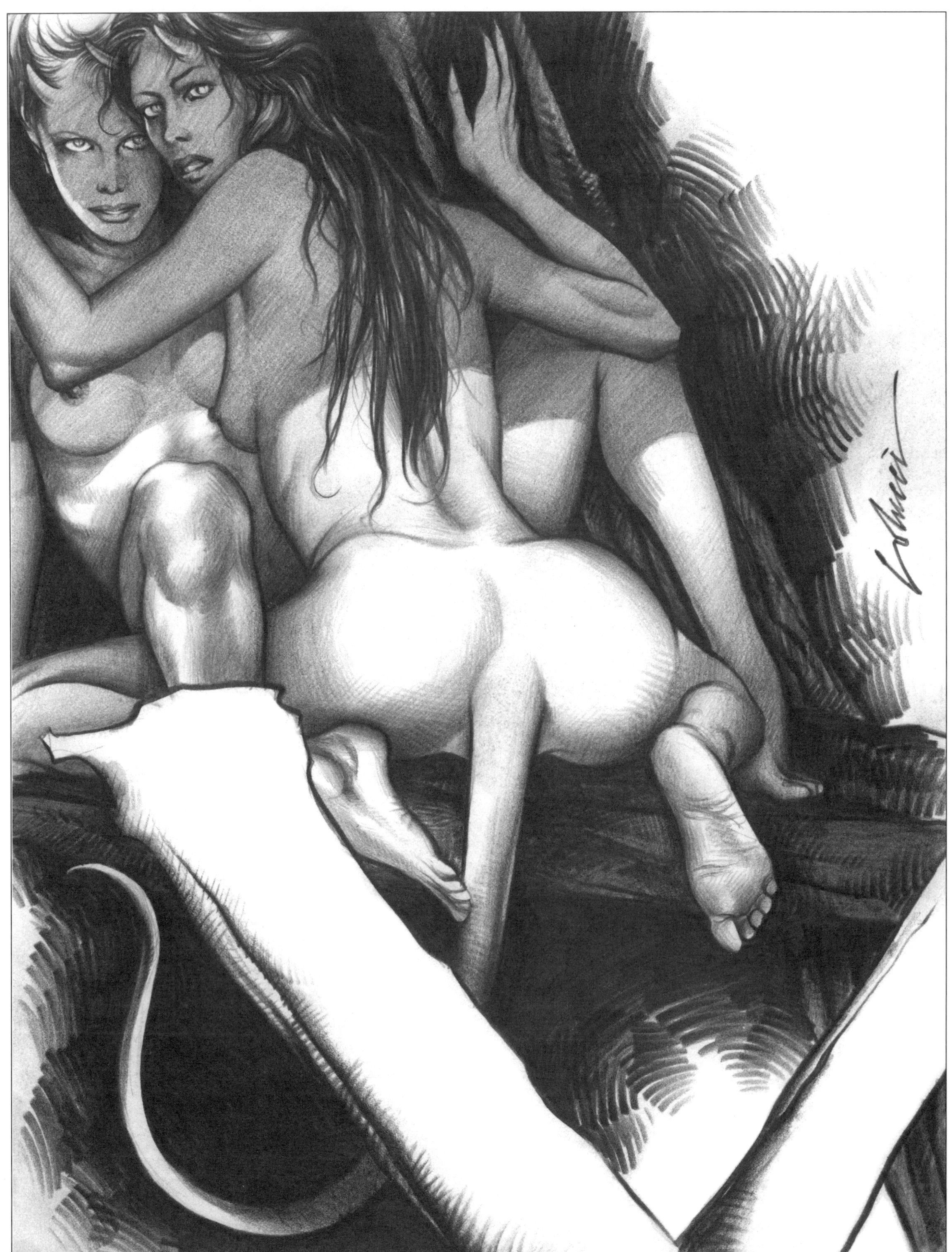

Alejandro Colucci